BUILD A WOR

EXCEPTIONAL

CONSISTENTLY EXCELLENT

EVERY

WEEK AFTER WEEK

SUNDAY

(NO MATTER WHO'S ON THE PLATFORM)

JON NICOL

©2023 Jon Nicol

All rights reserved.

No part of this book may be reproduced, stored in a retrieval system, or transmitted in any form or by any means, electronic, mechanical, photocopying, recording, or otherwise, without the prior written permission of the author, except as provided by U.S.A. copyright law.

Dedicated to the memory of my friend, Chris Skelnick.

Chris died unexpectedly while I was working on this book. I could write pages about his generous friendship and how much he encouraged me (usually over gyros at our local Greek restaurant).

I was looking forward to getting his take on this book when I finished.

I miss you, Chris.

CONTENTS

An Introduction (You'll Actually Want to Read) 1

Chapter i. The "I Can't Believe He Said That" Introduction 3

Chapter ii. Who This Book is For (And Who Should Ask for a Refund). 7

Chapter iii. How to Read this Book 17

Part 1: The Problem With Sunday. 23

Chapter 1. Reality Check. 25

Chapter 2. An Extra Crispy Worship Leader. 37

Chapter 3. Sunday-Driven Management 45

Part 2: Exceptional Sundays. 55

Chapter 4. The E4 Paradox. 57

Chapter 5. Exceptional Every Sunday Explained. 73

Chapter 6. Barriers to Exceptional Sundays. 91

Part 3: CAPACITY (How to Have Enough Time & Energy to Transform Your Team) 105

Chapter 7. Essential Capacity Leadership 107

Chapter 8. Simplify Sunday Planning 115

Chapter 9.   Build Supportive Structures .131

Chapter 10. Triple Your Time Off 147

Part 4: CULTURE (How to Create a Culture that Pursues Excellence). 157

Chapter 11. Creating Culture
  (Or, How to Nail Jello to a Wall) 159

Chapter 12. Clarify Compelling Vision .167

Chapter 13. Create Vision-Driven Expectations 183

Chapter 14. Uphold Loving Standards. 197

Part 5: CAPABILITIES (Get Your Team to Look & Sound Exceptional Every Sunday) 219

Chapter 15. Levels of Engagement 221

Chapter 16. Cultivate Musical Excellence 233

Chapter 17. Develop Platform Presence. 251

Chapter 18. Deepen Your Bench 263

Chapter 19. The Path To to Loving Better. 289

The Exciting Conclusion (Or, Just the Beginning…?) 299

Chapter 20. When Will YOU Skip Easter?. 301

Chapter 21. Seriously, What's Next?? .309

About the Author 313

An Introduction

(YOU'LL ACTUALLY WANT TO READ)

Chapter 1

THE "I CAN'T BELIEVE HE SAID THAT" INTRODUCTION

Honesty is the first chapter in the book of wisdom.

Thomas Jefferson

Full Disclosure

This book exists for two reasons:

Reason #1: So that you'll eventually work with my team and me to help you implement everything you read here.

Reason #2: To get you results in advance so that you'll want to do Reason #1 as quickly as possible.

You might be surprised that I said that. Most people would expect something more altruistic-sounding. Like, "To help as many worship leaders as possible build healthy worship ministries."

Yes, that's what I want to do. But the quickest and best way to that goal is through the kind of help we give in our coaching program.

THE "I CAN'T BELIEVE HE SAID THAT" INTRODUCTION

My team and I can help you build a worship team that…

- makes every Sunday exceptional…
- no matter who's scheduled, and…
- without burning out you or your team.

I know not every leader who picks up this book will pursue (or even want) the kind of focused help my team and I offer.

And I still want to help that leader. That's why I promise to show you what it takes to build a worship team that makes every Sunday exceptional… within the confines of a book you can easily digest in a few short hours.

I've packed tons of practical and tactical content in these pages. And, I've put in content about big-picture strategies as well.

I want to help you start the journey towards exceptional Sundays, so you can see what's possible.

Then, if we work together, we'll improve your worship ministry to a level that'd be tough to get to through DIY efforts. And, we'll help you get there at a pace that would be impossible on your own.

Throughout these pages, I will continue to be fully transparent, honest, and even blunt with you about…

1. What's possible and what's not.

I won't promise you a Tesla Model S and deliver a Kia Rio. Instead, I'll be realistic about what you can expect to improve on your own and what will be challenging if you go it alone.

2. My own mistakes, failings, and flailings.

I'll shoot straight about my many blunders so you can avoid them. As it turns out, I'm pretty darn good at transforming my mistakes into ministry-improving lessons. (That is, after a short span of blaming others and feeling sorry for myself).

3. My own success as a leader and a coach.

I want to be honest about my success as a full-time, vocational worship leader.

However, I won't sensationalize my success. For example, I'll tell you right now I was never famous as a worship leader. (Other than being famous in my own church for forgetting the words to songs – even ones I wrote.)

And I never served at a church you've heard of – unless you happen to live near Mansfield, Ohio.

But that's a big part of the reason people listen to me. I was a regular worship leader at a regular church with all the regular problems. And I worked hard and got help to overcome them.

When I talk about my successes, it's definitely not to brag. I just want to share what worked for me when I was leading a worship ministry and what's working now for my clients as they implement this ministry model.

Here's How This Book Works...

First, we'll talk about the big barriers and problems keeping you from growing the consistently excellent worship ministry you've always dreamed about.

THE "I CAN'T BELIEVE HE SAID THAT" INTRODUCTION

Next, I'll give you a detailed "insider's look" at the Exceptional Every Sunday Model.

Until now, I've never given anyone outside our private coaching group this many practical, how-to details.

For that reason, I recommend you read the book cover to cover.

BUT... because I know my people (worship leaders, artists, creatives), feel free to scan, skim, and then study in-depth whatever grabs your attention.

This model will help you transform your ministry in three critical areas:

1. Time (how to have enough of it)
2. Culture (how to make it about more than just excellence)
3. Development (how to equip your team to be consistently exceptional)

Finally, as we break down each part of the Exceptional Every Sunday Model, I'll give you practical how-tos and steps to get results in advance.

As you start to see the possibilities and achieve success on your own, I know you're someone who can go even further and faster through our coaching program.

Speaking of knowing you're someone I can help, in the following short chapter, I get specific about who this book is for and who should ask for a refund. (Because I'll give it to you if you're not a good fit.)

Chapter ii

WHO THIS BOOK IS FOR
(AND WHO SHOULD ASK FOR A REFUND)

Even if you're on the right track, you'll get run over if you just sit there.
Will Rogers

This Book is For You, If...

Before you invest any more time in this book, let me clarify who this book is for and who it's not for.

I don't want to waste your time if it's not for you. You might be one (or more) of these seven kinds of leaders. If you are, keep reading. This book is for you.

1. The "Sunday Grind" Leader

If you're this leader, you're tired of the Sunday grind. You've been in a cycle of meeting the demands of Sunday week after week, month after month, year after year.

And you're feeling "the grind."

WHO THIS BOOK IS FOR (AND WHO SHOULD ASK FOR A REFUND)

You might not be ready to give up. And you might not feel completely burned out. But there's a sense of fatigue that never used to be there.

Maybe you've only been doing ministry for a few years. Or perhaps you've been doing it for many years. But regardless, you're feeling the wear and tear of Sunday after Sunday after Sunday.

This book will help you get off the week-to-week treadmill, build beyond this Sunday, and lead at a sustainable pace for the long haul.

2. The "Lead Differently" Leader

The next leader this book is for is those who want to lead differently. If that's you, you've understood for a while that leading a worship ministry should go far beyond just getting ready for Sunday.

You want to grow your team numerically and develop them musically. But you also want to see them grow relationally and spiritually. More than ever, you've been thinking about discipleship and leadership development.

You want to take the counter-intuitive wisdom of scriptures like Ephesians 4:11-12 seriously. Leaders aren't doing the work of ministry themselves; they're equipping others to do the work – and they're sharing leadership.

You understand what you need to do. But the high demands of Sunday make implementing this kind of leadership difficult. As a result, you're hungry to find something to help you transition towards a more life-giving approach to ministry leadership.

3. The "Tired of Flying Solo" Leader

The typical worship leader flies solo in too many areas of their ministry. They're "the One" – the worship guy, the worship girl. That person who's up there every Sunday or who's running every part of the ministry. Eventually, this leader hits a wall if nothing changes.

If that's you, if you're…

- tired of being "the one"
- frustrated with flying solo
- fatigued from carrying the weight of the entire ministry

… this book is for you.

Also, if you've been the worship guy or girl in your church for a while, you've probably experienced the dark side of being "the one."

Even though you enjoy being upfront and leading every Sunday…

- It's tough to take time off. (We'll talk about this in depth later in the book.)

- You can't work ON your ministry because you're so busy working IN it. (We'll talk about this concept more, too.)

- And worst of all, your church has an unhealthy dependence on you. (We'll definitely talk about this issue.)

I'll show you a healthier model of leadership. You'll see a path to develop other leaders to share the Sunday load.

And, you'll learn a model where others help you do more than just lead Sunday. You can start sharing leadership in every area of your ministry.

WHO THIS BOOK IS FOR (AND WHO SHOULD ASK FOR A REFUND)

4. The "New Leader" Leader

The next person this book is for is the leader who's just starting in a new church or brand new to worship ministry.

You want to build the right foundations and structures that will not only strengthen your current ministry, but serve your church for years to come – even after you're long gone.

And, if you're just starting off, you'll gain the knowledge and skills that will propel you light years ahead of leaders who just figure things out as they go along.

This book is going to do that. It will help you put things in place now that I didn't discover until almost a decade of vocational worship leading.

In fact, I probably need to apologize to scores of team members and congregants from those early days. I inflicted more than my share of immature leadership.

5. The "I'm Drowning" Worship Leader

The next worship leader is the one who just might lose their job if something doesn't change. Either they'll quit because they're so overwhelmed, or they're at risk of getting fired because they're not meeting expectations.

I've talked to many worship leaders who were given a mandate – improve or move on.

Their senior pastor or leadership board gives them a job performance review with a litany of issues that need to be addressed. Some of these expectations might even feel unrealistic.

I feel for these leaders. Most went into worship leading because they love leading people in worship and enjoy making music. Suddenly they're expected to do all these administrative tasks while trying to improve and grow a team of volunteers.

They're overwhelmed.

If that's you, keep reading this book. These principles and practical steps will put you on the right path.

You'll become the kind of leader who produces exceptional Sundays and successfully overcomes the administrative barriers that trip up almost every worship leader.

6. The "I'm Leading a Worship Leader" Leader

I often work with senior, lead, and executive pastors looking for something to help them deveop their worship leaders. If that's you, you might face a few different challenges.

You might have a worship leader who's highly creative and musically talented. But he's also highly disorganized and administratively challenged.

Or, maybe you have a solid worship ministry coordinator, but she just can't maintain the standard of excellence you want for Sundays. The services don't feel creative and aren't really leading people on a journey of worship. It's just song after song.

Maybe your leader is getting older and less in touch with modern music. While he's a good leader and has a solid rapport with the team, you're afraid you may lose the next generation if he keeps your church on the current style trajectory.

WHO THIS BOOK IS FOR (AND WHO SHOULD ASK FOR A REFUND)

Or, maybe you've got a solid worship leader with plenty of leadership potential. But she's young and green. You can mentor her in a lot of aspects of ministry and leadership, but she also needs a guide who knows worship ministry.

If any of these fit the worship leader you're leading, keep reading this book.

You'll find a model of worship ministry that will...

- Help the administratively-challenge worship leader learn how to leverage systems and processes to run an organized team.
- Give the less-than-creative leader ways to upscale the Sunday experience and learn to tap into others' creativity.
- Empower your older worship leader to embrace the role of equipping and developing the next generation of worship leaders.
- Create solid foundations for your young worship leader to learn to lead a team and avoid so many of the typical mistakes newbie worship leaders make.

After you explore this model, let's set up a time to talk to see how my team and I can help your worship leader grow.

7. The "Looking for the Next Leader" Leader

Finally, the seventh kind of leader who will find this book invaluable is the one who wants to build an intentional succession plan.

If that's you, maybe you'd like to step down, transition, or retire in the next one to two years.

Or, perhaps you just feel your season at this particular church is ending, and you want to leave well. And so you're thinking about a succession plan.

Or, you might be the kind of leader who is just that forward-thinking. You want an intentional, long-term path toward a seamless handoff.

Regardless of your situation, you know that you'll leave sooner or later. But you don't want the typical transition to happen:

1. The current worship leader leaves.
2. The team pulls together with an interim leader, trying to keep the wheels on the bus.
3. A new leader is hired or appointed.
4. She implements a new program or approach to ministry (along with new songs).
5. The team struggles to get on board.
6. Eventually, the new leader and team members get on the same page after a little too much drama.
7. Then, the worship leader leaves.

This cycle goes on and on for too many churches. You can be the leader who breaks this cycle by saying enough is enough and work to build a healthy ministry that lasts far beyond you.

I trust you see yourself as one or more of those seven types of leaders. If you don't, you may need to keep reading to see if you're one of the types of worship leaders who should ask for a refund.

WHO THIS BOOK IS FOR (AND WHO SHOULD ASK FOR A REFUND)

This Book Is NOT For You If...

I'm not being snarky when I mentioned giving a refund. Even though this book is inexpensive, I don't want leaders spending their money (or wasting their time) on something they won't or can't use.

So let's take a look at who this book is *not* for.

1."Quick Fix" Leaders

This book is not for leaders who want quick-fix solutions. You're in the wrong place if you want something you can plug and play to get fast results.

Now, there are some concepts, tactics, and steps that I'll teach that will give you immediate results. And they're effective. But they're only part of the solution.

If you want to build a worship team that can be exceptional every Sunday, week after week, month after month, year after year, it's going to take more than just a few quick steps or fast tactics.

This book will deliver some quick gains. But to build a team that can make every Sunday exceptional, you have to play the long game.

2. "Easy-Button" Leaders

As I mentioned, this book has tangible, practical stuff you can use right now. But it's not sparkly unicorn dandruff that someone can just sprinkle over their ministry to make it magically grow. Leaders who want to implement this Exceptional Every Sunday Model need to gear up for a challenge.

But you know what? My guess is this...

You're already working hard!

You're already putting in the blood, sweat, and tears. Because of that, I want to make sure that those proverbial (and literal) bodily fluids are not shed in vain.

What I outline in this book will ensure your hard work is directed toward what will make a lasting change in your ministry for years to come.

3. "Special Snowflake" Leaders

The third person that this book is not for is the special snowflake.

Every worship leader has their own unique set of challenges. Likewise, every church has a particular set of circumstances that make leading more difficult than in other churches. At least, that's what we're all tempted to think as we look at the supposedly greener grass of other worship ministries.

But that's the kiss of death for true transformation – assuming "it won't work for me."

I don't know every challenge your church is facing. My coaches and I have maybe not encountered a team culture like yours.

But, here's what I do know. I've worked with worship leaders of different backgrounds, denominations, ages, sizes of churches, and levels of leadership experience. The one thing they have in common is this:

They didn't fall into the trap of thinking "this won't work for me."

Instead, they looked at how they could apply these Exceptional Every Sunday principles to their unique ministry to make it work.

WHO THIS BOOK IS FOR (AND WHO SHOULD ASK FOR A REFUND)

And that's why we offer coaching. We can't make a one-size-fits-all program. But we can walk alongside you to help you...

- Implement this model into your unique worship ministry.
- Leverage your special situation circumstances.
- Overcome your one-of-a-kind challenges.

I hope you don't find yourself as one of these leaders. But, chances are, if you've read this far into the book, you're the kind of leader who will choose to do great things with what you're about to discover here.

Chapter iii

HOW TO READ THIS BOOK

Sometimes incompetence is useful. It helps you keep an open mind.
Roberto Cavalli

The Wide Middle

In everything we do at WorshipTeamCoach.com, we strive to talk to the "wide middle"[1] of churches who employ or appoint…

- worship leaders…
- music ministers…
- worship pastors…
- worship and arts directors…

…and any number of titles that a church might bestow upon the person who leads their worship and music ministry.

---

[1] From our coaching program, membership site, standalone courses, blog posts, free webinars, etc., it's all designed to benefit churches in the "wide middle."

HOW TO READ THIS BOOK

I've worked with Catholics and Protestants, mainlines and 'non-denoms', evangelicals and Pentecostals, charismatics and baptists, more theologically conservative folks, and less theologically conservative folks.

The common denominator is that all these churches love God and want to worship the way they feel called to.

Because of that, I've designed this model to let you define what an "exceptional Sunday" looks like for you and your unique context.

Also, our framework, strategies, and tactics are designed to be as 'style-agnostic' as possible.

If you're rocking a 30-person choir and pipe organ every week, fantastic! This approach will help you build a team that can make every Sunday exceptional.

If you're a multi-campus, non-denominational "charisbaptist" church that likes the uniformity of running tracks and loops, great! This approach will help you build a team that can make every Sunday exceptional (at every campus).

If you're a biker church that meets in a VFW hall and your drummer has a double kick drum, please send me your service times and address. I want to visit. Also, this approach will help you build a team that can make every Sunday exceptional.

If you scan this book and DON'T think this model will help your church, shoot me an email and let's talk. You might be right. Or, you might be surprised. Either way, let's both keep an open mind.

He Said / She Said

Since worship leaders come in both varieties – men and women – I include both. But, I hope to avoid using the "slash and attach" method of he/she and him/her. That gets cumbersome to read and write.

So, I'll sometimes refer to worship leaders with the pronouns *she* and *her*, and sometimes with the pronouns *he* or *him*. And occasionally, if my editor lets me get away with it, I may slip in the *they* and *them* as singular pronouns – basically saying that this could apply to both the male leader and the female leader.

Building the Ministry You've Always Dreamed Of Leading

As I said earlier, each chapter contains actionable and practical content. Some of it you can put into practice immediately. Other steps may take a little time.

There might be the DIY-er who methodically works through this book to apply everything she can. That's fantastic!

Or, there might be the skimmer who scans this book to find nuggets of wisdom or tactics to add to his leadership toolbox. That's great, too.

I want you to get results and put this method to the test.

Ultimately, I hope you're the leader who says, "I want to implement this model for my worship ministry at a level and pace that would be almost impossible on my own."

HOW TO READ THIS BOOK

When you get to that place, whether it's after skimming a couple of chapters or reading the whole book cover to cover, let's talk!

That's what my team and I love doing – helping worship leaders build the kind of ministry that can make every Sunday exceptional, no matter who's scheduled, and without burning out themselves or their team.

We want to help you build the kind of worship ministry you've always dreamed of leading!

Here's to the exceptional success of you and your worship team,

Jon Nicol
WorshipTeamCoach.com
WorshipWorkshop.com

The Exceptional Sunday Assessment

When you're ready to explore what it would be like to work with my team and me, schedule an Exceptional Sunday Assessment.

During this one-on-one session, you and a coach will...

1. Take a look at how well your team is producing excellent Sundays, and we'll see what's working and what's not.
2. Identify some areas where you can raise your team's standard of excellence on and off the platform over the next 90 days and beyond.
3. Uncover the #1 issue holding your team back from sounding fantastic and being engaging lead worshipers consistently.
4. Develop a 3-step action plan that will help you make every Sunday exceptional ASAP.

Even if you decide it's not the right time or best fit to work with my team, you'll get tremendous amounts of clarity and value from this call.

There's no cost to you for this session, and you can schedule it here:

> https://www.worshipteamcoach.com/book-esa

Part 1

THE PROBLEM WITH SUNDAY

Chapter 1

REALITY CHECK

Reality is merely an illusion, albeit a very persistent one.
Albert Einstein

You, *worship leader… worship pastor… music minister* – whatever your title – face a unique challenge.

Your Sunday work…

> *The planning*
> *The scheduling*
> *The communication*
> *The preparation*
> *The last-minute cancellations*
> *The stage set-up*
> *The rehearsal*
> *The sound check*
> *The service*
> *The tear-down/clean up*

…happens every… single… week.

REALITY CHECK

Over and over, Sunday arrives every seven days with alarming regularity.

And as soon as one service is in the can, you gotta start working on another.

Also, the most significant part of your job performance is judged on a 20-minute set of music once a week:

- The quality depends on volunteers – all of which are a mixed bag of talent, experience, commitment, and maturity.
- Also, your job is critiqued by 100, 200, 700, 1500, or however many people attend your church. And every single one of them has opinions about what worship and church music should sound like.
- Those opinions are typically based on watching celebrity church services online. You know, the churches whose *weekly* production costs exceed your *annual* ministry budget. Heck, maybe even your *entire church's* annual budget.
- Few (if no one) can do what you do. Regardless, some are willing to share their opinions freely through notes or post-service comments.
- After you get through Sunday, you know your work will be dissected and picked apart in the Tuesday post-mortem – er, staff meeting.
- Meanwhile, you're already knee-deep in getting ready for this coming Sunday.

Over and over goes this *wash, rinse, repeat* pattern of churning out worship services. And amid those recurring weekly demands, you know that making Sunday special isn't just accomplished with planning and rehearsals.

To maintain and improve Sunday standards, you have to somehow get that team of volunteers to *sound better*, *look better*, and *love better*. (More on these three ideas later.)

And this is NOT easy. You're dealing with a mixed bag of volunteer musicians:

- Most are extremely busy (and like to remind you just *how* busy they are).
- They also demonstrate various levels of commitment (and it's rarely the level you desire).
- Some are untrained in critical areas of musicianship or technical skills.
- Some are newer and still need to get up to speed. They're a bit of an anchor for you, but you love their enthusiasm.
- Some are older and stuck in their ways. They're also an *anchor*, but without the enthusiasm.

Besides their vastly different skill, commitment, and maturity levels, you also have to deal with varying personality types.

- Some are amiable and 'go along to get along.'
- Some are task-oriented. They just want to get down to business and get home.
- Some are direct and assertive. You feel like they might be challenging your authority.

REALITY CHECK

- And some just want to make every rehearsal and soundcheck a party – with themselves at the center of attention.

And the tension doesn't stop there.

You're not just a *worship leader* – the person responsible for planning and leading Sunday.[2]

You are a *Worship Ministry Leader*.

You run a complex organization staffed with volunteers who you need to develop musically, technically, relationally, and even spiritually.

To lead this team and successfully produce Sunday services, you are responsible for running or overseeing several structures, processes, and systems that keep the ministry running:

- Scheduling
- Service Planning
- Music Distribution
- Song Management
- Rehearsals / Sound Checks
- Tech / Production
- Team Communications
- Team Member Development
- Leadership Development
- New Team Member Acquisition

---

[2] There are a few lucky leaders – usually in larger churches – who get to focus most of their attention on just making Sunday amazing. All the administrative work and team development is someone else's job. If you're reading this book, that's probably not your situation.

And that's just in the worship ministry area. If a smaller or medium size church employs you, you may wear other leadership hats…

- Student Ministry
- Small Groups
- Video / Graphic Design / Marketing
- Family or Children Ministry
- Outreach

And then there's that pesky line in your job description, *"And any other responsibilities deemed necessary by the senior pastor."*

Oh, and I forgot to mention. Each year, two major holidays will demand unreasonable expectations for high production and extra services to impress people who only come to church twice every 12 months.

Am I getting close to describing your situation?

You're in the *Worship Leader Crazy Cycle*.

The Crazy Cycle

Most worship leaders get stuck in this cycle by focusing on the urgent work to get through Sunday after Sunday after Sunday.

Because of that, they only dabble in the non-urgent work of developing their team members, growing leaders, and building healthy ministry structures and processes.

And inside the crazy cycle are four 'sub-cycles' that make this problem even more complex.

REALITY CHECK

The Exhausted Cycle

After too long of primarily focusing on Sunday demands, worship leaders realize they're doing it all themselves.

They haven't equipped other leaders or core team members to help carry out the work of the ministry. That lack of help and support compounds week after week, month after month, year after year until, one day, they hit a wall.

Now, this Exhausted Cycle is sneaky. You can go round and round on it for years at various levels of fatigue and avoid a full-tilt burnout. But, even the low levels of exhaustion keep you from investing the time and energy into developing your worship ministry for the long term.

And rest assured, if you stay on this cycle, you'll one day experience the soul-crushing exhaustion of burnout. Maybe not soon, but someday.

The Enabling Cycle

Because of Sunday demands and too little focus on development, worship leaders *enable* their team members to stay at low levels of semi-committed and self-focused behavior.

This self-focused and semi-committed behavior might include…

- Showing up late
- Last minute call-offs
- No-showing for rehearsal
- Not practicing enough
- Entitlement and other attitude issues

And all this frustrating behavior makes your job even harder.

But, when the urgent demands of Sunday are breathing down your neck, it's easier just to let that stuff slide than try to tackle the root cause of it.

The Entrenched Cycle

The Crazy Cycle makes you feel like you can't get out of it because Sunday requires so much time and focus.

It feels like you can never take enough time away from Sunday work to develop your worship ministry for the long term. Or, if you did invest that time, the quality of Sunday would drop, and your job would be on the line.

You feel *stuck*.

The Erosive Cycle

There's also a continual *erosion* going on in your ministry.

Because you have to spend so much time on maintaining your Sunday service standards, your team's spiritual and relational health often erodes and deteriorates.

The semi-committed and self-focused behavior isn't just an issue with a few people. It becomes part of your team's culture:

- Preparation isn't a priority.
- Team members act entitled and get territorial about their positions and parts.
- Gossip, sarcasm, and other corrosive language are allowed to go unchecked.

REALITY CHECK

- Those pursuing spiritual growth and demonstrating maturity are the outliers – and they're finding themselves more and more repelled by the team culture.

The worship leader in this Erosive Cycle risks losing good people, further deteriorating the culture.

Where Are You?

You might not yet be at a place where you see or feel all the effects of the Crazy Cycle. But if you've been leading worship for more than a couple of years, you're probably starting to experience some of the tension.

I want to help you escape the Crazy Cycle before it wreaks havoc on you, your family, and your worship team.

On the other hand, you might be feeling every bit of that endless Crazy Cycle. And because of those demands of Sunday after Sunday, you don't see a way out of this any time soon.

In fact, buying this book might have been a last-ditch effort before you give it all up to deliver packages for Amazon.

You may or may not be considering a career switch to a last-mile delivery driver. But if you're feeling entrenched and exhausted, I want to help you break free from this cycle of 'death by ministry.'

Why Do We Do This??

Because of the complex nature of leading a church worship and music program, it's no wonder that most leaders default to focusing on *this Sunday* and *next Sunday*. Unfortunately, this leaves little time for their team's long-term development and other ministry improvements.

Whether they're volunteer, part-time, or full-time, it doesn't matter. Most worship leaders fall into that vicious cycle of Sunday-driven management. Because of that, any growth or improvement for the team is accidental. Or it may come at the expense of overtime hours (for which the leader is rarely ever compensated financially).

Now, I've painted a bleak picture. Someone from the outside might ask, "Why would anyone want to do this job??"

Because we LOVE it!! *Right??*

We're all drawn to worship leadership by one or more of these things…

- Worshiping God through music
- Leading others in the worship experience
- Making music with other people
- Creating and planning meaningful setlists
- Writing or arranging worship songs
- Shepherding and loving people
- Developing and leading a team

…and more.

If you're still at a place where the 'I LOVE IT' stuff outweighs the 'I JUST GOTTA DO THIS' stuff, that's awesome!

My goal is to help you build your worship ministry so that you can continually lean into your strengths and passion. And I'll help you

REALITY CHECK

develop systems, processes, and people to enable you to lead the areas that aren't in your wheelhouse.

Now, if the never-ending Sunday cycle has worn you down, and the joy of the 'I LOVE IT' stuff doesn't offset the drudgery of 'I JUST GOTTA DO THIS' stuff, take courage.

I've been there, and I want to help you.

So please keep reading, and I'll walk with you on a path to recover your passion for leading your worship team and growing your ministry – in a way that's life-giving once again for you.

Are you feeling stuck?

If you feel stuck and you've lost some of your love for ministry, schedule an Exceptional Sunday Assessment. During this call, you and a coach will talk about…

- The goals you have for your team and yourself…
- Where you're at right now…
- And what might be holding you back from reaching your goals.

Even if you decide it's not the right time or best fit to work with my team, you'll get tremendous amounts of clarity and value from this call.

There's no cost to you for this session, and you can schedule it here:

https://www.worshipteamcoach.com/book-esa

Chapter 2

AN EXTRA CRISPY WORSHIP LEADER

Ministry burnout is a real problem because it's never-ending.
Tony Evans

I felt like a failure.

It was the end of 2008, and I had been in ministry for a decade. The church I worked at was taking a financial beating because of the Great Recession. They realized they could no longer afford two full-time staff.

Here's a fun lesson: the worship guy is far more dispensable than the senior pastor.

But that's not why I felt like a failure.

When I found out I only had two more months at that church, I remember thinking, *"All I'm leaving behind here is a stack of Sunday setlists."*

AN EXTRA CRISPY WORSHIP LEADER

I hadn't developed anyone to lead, plan, or coordinate the worship ministry. And I had no systems in place that DIDN'T require me.

> Scheduling
> Auditioning
> Song rotation / song management
> Mentoring & training musicians
> Set / service planning
> Musical directing & arranging
> Shepherding / care of the team
> Creating and casting vision

I did it all. 100%!

And leadership development? I did a little… but only enough for someone to take my place while I was on vacation. So I led 50 out of 52 weeks, plus special holiday services.[3]

Because of my short-sighted leadership, the musical quality of that church suffered for a while after I left.

Why?

I fell for the "Sunday Trap."

I had focused 99% of my energy and time on the quality of "This Sunday." And you know all too well what comes after "This Sunday"…

Another "This Sunday."

Since I poured most of my energy into the demands of "this Sunday" week after week,

---

[3] I probably would've led the other two weeks but my wife made me take a vacation.

- The band relied on me to hold it together.
- The vocalists didn't know how to be engaging lead worshipers.
- And no one else knew how to plan song sets that led the congregation on an intentional journey of worship.

"So, is there a happy ending anywhere in this story, Jon?" you might be wondering.

Yes. But not yet.

Early in 2009, I got hired at another church. That was an even bigger mess.

The previous leader had been gone for months, and a committee was now leading the team.

(May God have mercy on any church whose worship ministry is led by a committee.)

The team sounded bad. They looked like a stage full of bored zombies (minus the rotting flesh). And there was a litany of commitment and attitude issues like…

- Very little personal practice
- Lateness to rehearsals and sound checks
- Last-minute cancellations or complete no-shows
- Bitterness and gossip
- Attitude issues and other self-focused behavior

And the icing on the cake? Roughly a third of the team didn't like me because I was so different from their former leader.

Over time, I started transforming this musically and relationally dysfunctional team:

- The music and worship sets were consistently high quality, week after week.
- The platform team was engaging and expressive.
- People prioritized personal practice and rehearsals.
- They showed up on time with their music learned.
- They responded to scheduling requests and took ownership when they couldn't make it.
- They even became more committed and respectful to one another – and me.

But I realized something.

I was falling into the same trap as before. Most of my improvements were about *this Sunday* – sounding better and looking better. I eventually found myself stuck in the endless Crazy Cycle we discussed in the last chapter.

And I wanted *out*.

Here's what happened next.

Extra Crispy

Eight men stared at me from around the boardroom table.

Their expressions ranged from skeptical to empathetic.

A few were poker-faced, not giving away what they were thinking. But at that moment, I didn't care what they thought.

I'd had enough.

At that point, I had been the worship pastor for about six years, having landed at this church after my Great Recession lay-off.

I did the math. Since starting a vocational ministry in my early to mid-20s, I had been responsible for planning and staffing at least 832 Sundays – and directly leading 752 of them. Probably more.

Sunday after Sunday after Sunday after Sunday...

During my six years at this church, every 12 - 18 months presented a new challenge:

The First Challenge:

Turn around a relationally and musically dysfunctional team, as I noted above.

The Second Challenge:

When I got hired, it was a two-campus church. So I had to grow the team to staff a comfortable rotation at both campuses.

When I started, most musicians played at both campuses each Sunday. It was a logistical nightmare.

The Third Challenge:

The church decided it wasn't operating the two-campus model very well. (I could have told them that a lot sooner, but who listens to the worship guy?)

The leadership determined they could serve their two widely different communities better as two different churches. So I was tasked with dividing my worship ministry to staff what was essentially two church plants.

The Fourth Challenge:

Rebuild the team at the campus – now a new church – that my family chose, saying goodbye to some fantastic team members and friends.

And the next challenge happened almost simultaneously with this fourth challenge.

The Fifth Challenge:

Renovate a former beer distributorship warehouse into a house of worship.

This meant going toe-to-toe with the building committee, architect, and contractor to get the layout and technology I knew the church needed. Had I not intervened, the stage would have been the dimensions of a queen-size mattress and the sound system purchased from RadioShack.

(OK, I exaggerate a little. But they were trying to go bare bones.)

The Sixth Challenge:

Now that we had a permanent space, it was time to move my team to in-ears and click tracks. Despite a slow and intentional process towards this, I lost a drummer and two singers on that move.

Amid all these seasons, I built a worship leader coaching business and launched a team member training site. Oh, and we went from two kids to four. (Not all at once, however.)

And through it all, I was planning, staffing, and leading… *Sunday after Sunday after Sunday after Sunday.*

"Do you smell something burning?"

Oh, that's just Jon.

Don't get me wrong. I loved tackling all those challenges. I'm NOT the guy you hire to maintain the status quo. I deliberately break things if I have to manage business as usual for too long.

But the work of building and rebuilding the ministry, growing a side hustle into a full-time job, and being responsible in some way for 52 Sundays a year eventually took its toll.

And there I sat in front of my church elders…

[cue heart-wrenchingly sad music… probably something by Sarah McLachlan]

…broken, burned out, and asking for a sabbatical.

Denied!

But I did get two extra weeks of vacation that year.

Gee… thanks, guys!

(Whether you're a vocational or volunteer worship leader, you know the work to take off for two weeks is hardly negated by the time off. So please forgive my sarcasm.)

After the board deep-sixed my sabbatical request, I had three options: quit, keep going, or find a different way to lead.

I thought about quitting and finding another church (not necessarily in that order). But I couldn't imagine starting over with another church. And chances are, it would mean uprooting my family to a new city. Short of a conversation with a burning bush, that was *not* going to happen.

I knew if I kept going on the same path and at the same pace, I wouldn't last another 18 months. So I had to choose door number three:

Find a different way to lead my worship ministry.

And that's what I'll show you in this book. But my goal for you is to get there faster and with fewer scars than I did.

Now, I got to tell you this:

It won't be easy.

It's hard work. But if you wanted easy, you would've been a youth pastor, right?[4]

---

[4] Just kidding, youth pastors. I was once one of you and know how tough your job is. So much so that I will never do that again.

Chapter 3

SUNDAY-DRIVEN MANAGEMENT

The manager accepts the status quo; the leader challenges it.
Warren Bennis

Let me ask you a few questions to get started with this chapter.

First question:

Do you remember in the first chapter when I reminded you that you're not *just* a worship leader but that you are, in fact, a worship *ministry* leader?

And do you remember that 'tip of the iceberg' list of all the stuff you need to do? Like…

- Scheduling
- Service Planning
- Music Distribution
- Song Management
- Rehearsals / Sound checks
- Tech / Production

- Team Communications
- Team Member Development
- Leadership Development
- New Team Member Acquisition

Yeah, sorry to remind you of all that. But hang with me here. I'm going to define this "*worship ministry leader*" role in a different way. You'll see why in a second.

Next question:

There is likely a senior leadership team above you, correct?

It looks a little different in every church. The senior pastor is almost always a part of it. And it might also include a governing board, an elder board, or an executive team that's a combination of pastors, directors, and/or elders.

Chances are, you're not on that leadership team. But you might be if you've reached that level of leadership experience. But most worship leaders aren't. (Even if you are, that executive role is usually in addition to your work as a worship ministry leader.)

Now, if you're not on the senior leadership team but a worship ministry leader, what does that make you?

A mid-level manager.

As a creative musician and artist, hearing that job title probably sucked away a portion of your soul.

I get it. It's the last thing most of us signed up for, right?

But the truth is, your job isn't just about putting on a weekend worship service.

- You have systems, structures, and processes to implement and maintain.
- You have volunteers to manage, train, and care for.
- And you have leaders to develop, deploy, and delegate to.

All the while, there's a senior leadership team above you who have expectations and standards they want you to meet. And sometimes, they might even make a few unrealistic demands because they don't understand the complex alchemy that goes into creating Sunday.

Welcome to middle-management! It's where the artist's soul goes to die.

> Take a moment.
> Breathe into a paper bag.
> Eat some ice cream.

Whatever it takes to process this traumatic realization.

But before you fall into despair or resign yourself to a life of drudgery, know this:

I'm going to show you how to be an amazing "Sunday manager" AND be able to lean into your artistry, creativity, and your passion areas that drew you to worship ministry in the first place.

But we first have to face this reality.

SUNDAY-DRIVEN MANAGEMENT

You ARE a Sunday Manager

It is true. You are, indeed, a Sunday manager. You have to coordinate multiple people, processes, and plans every week.

Take a moment to think about everything you do to make Sunday successful.

- Plan music sets and service orders.
- Communicate those sets with your band and techs.
- Change sets and service orders because the senior pastor wants to add something else to the service. (*On Saturday!*)
- Apologize to your team because you've had to change the setlist… *again*.
- Schedule team members.
- Follow up with team members when they still have a yellow question mark next to their name the day before rehearsal.
- Find replacements for those with yellow question marks who "just realized" they have to go out of town.
- Create or compile charts, recordings, and other resources to help your team prepare.
- Communicate with your team and distribute the charts, recordings, and other resources.
- Rehearse the team.
- Make in-the-moment decisions to change arrangements when things aren't working.
- Coordinate with the lighting, graphics, video, and sound techs.
- Run a warm-up and sound check.

- Tackle last-minute changes or issues that arise.
- Lead a service. Or two. Or three.
- Field requests for new songs from people in the congregation. Or worse, the senior pastor.[5]
- Deal with complaints about volume, song choices, and skirt lengths.
- Attend a staff meeting to hear how well (or poorly) you did on Sunday from a group of people who are vastly unqualified to do your job.
- And then, start it all over for *next* Sunday.

We could quadruple this already absurd list with a few minutes together brainstorming. But regardless of how long a list like this is, your church *needs* good Sunday management.

So that means they also need a wildly good Sunday manager to pull it off week after week.

And that's YOU!

Don't hear me wrong – you don't have to be the "100% BEST" at everything Sunday management requires. No one can be.

But I am saying you need to be "100% RESPONSIBLE" for delivering the demands of Sunday.

And I will show you how to do that while still being able…

- Take enough time off.
- Grow additional leaders.

---

[5] Does it ever feel like people think you're their Sunday morning jukebox? Yeah, me too.

- Develop and train team members.
- Reserve time for your passion projects.

Later in this book, we'll discuss how to create structures and systems that enable you to finish your work excellently but in less time. That is, how to be a world-class manager of Sundays.

But before we do that, we need to debunk a false belief that most worship leaders buy into.

Succumbing to Sunday Demands

The false belief is this:

As the worship leader, I need to prioritize Sunday services above all else.

Like I said in a previous chapter, there are worship leaders in some huge churches whose only mandate is to make Sunday unforgettable. They are part of a multi-person worship staff larger than many churches.

You're probably not one of those leaders. Again, you're a Sunday manager.

But the insidious nature of that false belief is this… it turns *Sunday managers* into *Sunday-driven managers*.

Sunday-driven managers fall into the trap of making Sunday morning the ultimate priority and fail to truly lead their teams beyond THIS SUNDAY.

A Sunday-driven manager will invest almost all their focus and energy into providing a good Sunday service week after week.

And the result?

They neglect the long-term growth and development of the worship ministry.

It's not just the organizational structure of the worship ministry that suffers.

- Disciples are not made, and leaders are not developed by Sunday-driven managers. Sunday-driven managers create *assistants* and *substitutes*, not *ministers* and *leaders*.
- "Leadership development" devolves into "how do I find a substitute for when I want to take a vacation?"
- And the lofty goal for "team development" is to get volunteers to show up to rehearsal with reasonable predictability and to sound good on Sunday.

I need to say it again: Sunday-driven managers…

- don't make disciples,
- don't develop leaders, and…
- don't grow the ministry beyond next Sunday.

The long-term effect of this Sunday-driven management is what we talked about earlier – the worship ministry *Crazy Cycle*.

The worship leader just keeps running and gunning Sunday after Sunday after Sunday and can't help but fall into those…

Exhausted…
Enabling…
Entrenched…

and

Erosive Cycles that we looked at in Chapter 1.

So what's the alternative to Sunday-driven management?

We'll look at that in the next chapter.

Sunday-Driven Manager?

If you feel stuck as a Sunday-driven manager and you want to get out of that rut, schedule an Exceptional Sunday Assessment. During this call, you and a coach will talk about…

- The goals you have for your team and yourself…
- Where you're at right now…
- And what might be holding you back from reaching your goals.

Even if you decide it's not the right time or best fit to work with my team, you'll get tremendous amounts of clarity and value from this call.

There's no cost to you for this session, and you can schedule it here:

https://www.worshipteamcoach.com/book-esa

Part 2
EXCEPTIONAL SUNDAYS

Chapter 4

THE E4 PARADOX

You take the red pill, you stay in wonderland, and I show you how deep the rabbit hole goes.
Morpheus

A Very Convincing Lie

Before we dive into E4 Leadership, I want to dive deeper into that Sunday-driven management lie we talked about in the last chapter:

As the worship leader, I need to prioritize Sunday services above all else.

This false belief is responsible for so much frustration and burnout for leaders, and even the mistreatment of worship team members.

Except, here's the reality for many worship leaders: *that statement doesn't sound false.*

The reason it doesn't sound false is because it's the narrative of most churches. It's NORMAL. That's just what we do.

Whether a person's title is worship pastor, worship leader, music minister, worship director, praise band leader, etc.…

…it's about making the Sunday worship service – primarily the musical portion – *excellent*.

In fact, a pastor or church might get a little panicked if their worship leader DOESN'T prioritize Sunday.

As a result, a majority of all vocational and volunteer worship ministry leaders are *Sunday-driven managers* leading *Sunday-driven teams*.

But I'm here to show you a different way. This is your *red pill / blue pill* moment.

(Yep, we're doing a Matrix illustration.)

Take the Red Pill

> *"You take the blue pill, the story ends, you wake up in your bed and believe whatever you want to believe. You take the red pill, you stay in wonderland, and I show you how deep the rabbit hole goes."*
>
> – Morpheus to Neo in *The Matrix*.

Too many worship leaders are content to take the blue pill and stay in the weekly cycle of Sunday-Driven Manager.

But…

- If you want to lead your team (and church) to a new level of excellence…
- If you want to build the kind of team you've only ever dreamed of leading…

EXCEPTIONAL EVERY SUNDAY

- If you want to get out of the crazy cycle of Sunday after Sunday...

... you've got to be subversive and go against what *most* worship leaders do.

- Most leaders can't take a Sunday off (without extensive pre-work).
- Most leaders are operating at low levels of functional exhaustion.
- Most leaders can't invest time into what they're passionate about (songwriting, arranging, special nights of worship, building relationships on the team, mentoring younger musicians, etc.).
- Most leaders dream of building a fantastic team (but have no idea how to do it).
- Most leaders' efforts to develop their team's musical skills are haphazard at best and result in little lasting change.
- Most worship leaders never go beyond surface-level relationships with more than a few people on their team. Sure, the team *gets along* but rarely *gets real*.
- Most leaders have resigned themselves to being stuck with the status quo of semi-committed team members with lukewarm spiritual maturity.
- Most leaders have become OK with a team that's OK with being OK.

And I could go on and on. But you're seeing it, right? If you want to grow the kind of worship team that can...

THE E4 PARADOX

- Make every Sunday look and sound exceptional…
- Regardless of who's scheduled…
- Without burning out you or your team…

Then you CAN'T be like most worship leaders.

It's time to lead differently.

It's time to subvert the system.

It's time to embrace E4 Leadership.

It's time to take the red pill.

What Is E4 Leadership?

So what is E4 Leadership? It's not a new gimmick or slick method. It's actually ancient leadership wisdom.

If we're going to be highly effective worship ministry leaders, we have to embrace the leadership lesson taught in Ephesians 4:11-12:

Now these are the gifts Christ gave to the church: the apostles, the prophets, the evangelists, and the pastors and teachers. Their responsibility is to equip God's people to do his work and build up the church, the body of Christ. (NLT)

E4 is our shorthand for leaders living out and applying the ancient approach to effective leadership. And we become E4 leaders when we embrace Ephesians 4:11-12.

Unfortunately, too many "Biblical" churches out there have missed the boat with Paul's concise leadership treatise here.

Most churches have hierarchical leadership structures that allow (and even encourage)...

- *Solo leadership.* Sure, there *are* multiple leaders, but each leader runs their own ministry, which leads to...
- *Siloed leadership.* Leaders in churches are sectioned off from each other via departments, even to the point of becoming territorial and competing for resources.
- *Top-down leadership.* Authority is hoarded rather than shared.

All this leaves "the work of ministry" to *the professionals* and only enlists "God's people" to be *assistants* in that work. Or if leadership is thrust upon volunteers, it's usually as a *substitute leader* with no long-term development plan.

While not every church has these issues to an extreme, most don't resemble the shared leadership and equipping focus of Ephesians 4:11-12. And because of that, worship ministries have become microcosms of their churches' unhealthy leadership structures.

The child mimics the parent.

The 4 Es of E4 Leadership

Nerd alert!

I couldn't have a concept like E4 leadership without giving you four Es.

But Boomer jokes aside (I'm Gen-X, thank you very much), these four Es will give you a framework for understanding, and more importantly, *applying* E4 Leadership into your worship ministry.

THE E4 PARADOX

Here are four Es for becoming an E4 leader.

ELEVATE

You need to elevate your view of Ephesians 4:11-12.

Taking an elevated view of Ephesians 4 means we should be about equipping team members and building other leaders – instead of doing the work of ministry ourselves.

This elevated view of Ephesians 4 requires a shift.

You need to make a shift…

- *From* putting almost all of your focus on the weekend services and doing most of the work of ministry yourself…
- *To* prioritizing your time to develop more engaged team members and move them towards equipped leadership.

This doesn't mean you spend all your time on leadership or team member development.

You'll likely still spend most of your time on Sunday. But, you'll intentionally invest focused chunks of time into team and leadership development.

It's a matter of a *priority shift*, not a large *quantity of time shift*.

Does that make sense?

If it doesn't, I'll show how in a moment. At the end of this chapter, I will give you a practical takeaway to help you make that shift. Remember, I told you I'm getting you results in this book, not just theories and ideas.

So, that's the first E. You need to ELEVATE your role from Sunday-driven manager to true Ephesians 4 equipping and discipling leader.

ENGAGE

The second E is about engaging your team in a journey of development – musical, spiritual, and relational. You're going to help your team *look better, sound better,* and *love better*. And again, in doing so, you create the kind of team that can make every Sunday exceptional.

In later chapters, we'll explore team member development more in-depth. But just know, as you're engaging them and leading them into training and development, you can do the third E.

EQUIP

You will be able to equip your team not only to do the work of ministry but also to grow to be leaders, mentors, and role models.

Not every person on your team should or will grow into an "official" leader on your team. But every healthy team member should be equipped for their highest level of service and ministry. At the very least, they'll be someone you can point to and say to a new person, "Follow their example."

Later, I'll give you a model for team development that shows you the growth path from the lowest levels of participation to the higher levels of ministry and leadership. But for now, let's talk about the final E.

EXPAND

As you embrace E4 leadership, you'll expand your team to a new level of exceptional (musically, relationally, and spiritually).

But the *Expand Phase* is more about you.

If you haven't already, you'll get a vision to expand from a *single leader* to *multiple leaders*. And ultimately, you'll embrace a leadership multiplication mindset that goes wildly beyond your own worship ministry and church. You'll see the expanding of leaders as a way for widespread Kingdom growth, not just building your own team.

Just take a second to imagine what that would be like in your ministry.

- Multiple worship leaders.
- A leadership team helping lead and manage the different areas of your worship ministry.
- Sending out equipped leaders to church plants and multiple campuses.
- Being able to hand off your ministry someday to someone you've raised up.

That was one of the greatest joys of my leadership at my last church. I prepared my ministry to go on without me by developing a successor and intentionally handing off the leadership reins.

It was tough. And messy. But it served the team and the church I had been investing in for most of a decade.

> **Want To Plan Your Succession?**
>
> If you'd like help learning what it takes to intentionally create a succession plan and develop your worship ministry successor, let's talk.
>
> Your first step is to schedule an Exceptional Sunday Assessment here:
>
> https://www.worshipteamcoach.com/book-esa

If we as leaders are to take Ephesians 4:11-12 seriously, along with scriptures like 2 Timothy 2:2, we can't just hold on to our leadership for years and then one day give a 30-day notice.

We are called as spiritual leaders to build up a process that continues far beyond us.

The E4 Paradox

Here's something I discovered after working for years to make each Sunday awesome and then pivoting towards being an E4 Leader.

When I focused on creating great Sundays every week, I created an OK team eventually. But when I worked to build an exceptional team, eventually, I couldn't help but have exceptional Sundays... every week.

It's what I call the *E4 Paradox*.

So much of my focus, time, and sweat went into making every Sunday experience a good one. And along the way, I built a decent team.

But when I shifted my priority from Sunday production to team development, I built a team that could consistently deliver the quality level I had always been striving for.

And I also discovered this: *I didn't have to work nearly as hard to make Sunday exceptional!*

When you jump down the rabbit hole of the E4 Paradox, you'll soon find the exit ramp for that Sunday-after-Sunday, never-ending expressway you're on right now.

A Practical Shift

Later in the book, there'll be more actionable content. But I don't want you to get beyond these early chapters without giving you something you can do right now to embrace E4 Leadership in a practical way.

First, you need to understand that shifting from a Sunday Driven Manager to an E4 Leader is a matter of…

1. An internal *attitude* shift in how you see yourself.

2. An external *priority* shift of what you focus on in your ministry.

These two shifts will help you move from Sunday-driven manager to E4 Leader.

Second, here's the practical takeaway to help you make this change:

Embrace and leverage Parkinson's law to prioritize and complete the *important* work before the *urgent* work.

I don't have time to get into the history and theory of Parkinson's law now, but the definition of it applied to task management is this:

Work expands to fill the time allowed for it.

A great example of Parkinson's law in action is when worship leaders hunt for the next fabulous new song.

Once every couple of months, I scoured PraiseCharts and the CCLI Charts listening to song after song. When I finished, I usually had a list of two or three "definites" and five or six "maybes."

Then, I'd look at the clock and realize it had taken me 3 hours and 12 minutes to find those songs.

I put no time restraints on that task. As a result, it ballooned out to consume my entire afternoon.

Once I learned about this hack, I set a timer for 45 minutes when searching for new songs. The time limit forced me to be more focused and make decisions quicker, so I could get through the mountain of new songs.

And I usually ended up with the same results – a couple of keepers and a few maybes. But I then had most of my afternoon still open.

So how do we use Parkinson's law to move toward E4 leadership?

There are lots of ways to use this law as a time-saving hack, but here's one big tactic:

Do E4 work first.

Rather than start your 'this Sunday' work on Monday morning (or whatever your first office day is), carve out anywhere from 5-10% of your week to work on a long-term ministry growth project.

THE E4 PARADOX

Let's look at an example of this.

Rachel Meets Parkinson

Rachel is a worship pastor at a larger church. Even with a full-time tech and an administrative assistant, she can't get done what she wants to get done.

Every week, the work of Sunday, staff meetings, and other ministry demands keep her running right up until Thursday night rehearsal. And too often, the work even splashes into her day off on Friday.

As she starts work each Monday, she often looks back over her previous week and realizes she made no progress on her dilapidated audition process.

She had slapped that process together in her first few months on the job since her predecessor's only standards were apparently, "Can fog a mirror and play four chords."

But even though her current qualification system is better than that, Rachel knows whenever someone says, "I'm interested," they're about to go through an inconsistent process that's different for each person.

Sick of reinventing the wheel for every new applicant, Rachel decides to try this "Parkinson's law hack."

She commits the first three hours of her week for the next couple of months to build out her new team member qualification process. And, within six weeks, voilà! She now has a streamlined and repeatable process to audition new team members.

Rachel applied Parkinson's law in two ways.

First, she limited this special project, so it didn't steal too much from her critical preparation for Sunday.

But that limitation had a benefit beyond just protecting the rest of her work week. The compressed time sharpened her focus, so she got more done than she expected on the project each week.

The second way she leveraged Parkinson's was to compress the time allowed for her 'Sunday work.'

Rachel typically invests around twenty office hours to get Sunday work done. Meetings, rehearsals, services, and such fill her remaining hours. She had unknowingly allowed her Sunday work to fill those twenty hours.

But now, she's intentionally compressed it to seventeen hours and found it's sufficient to complete her Sunday work.

Tighter time constraints force a tighter focus.

As You Make The Shift

So, do you see how making a 5 - 10% tweak in your schedule can help you make that shift toward E4 leadership?

As you make that shift, you'll have...

- More time to build the ministry systems that allow you to become a more effective E4 leader. (More on that in a later chapter.)
- More time to invest in your passion projects.
  And...
- More time off to invest in your family and emotional health.

THE E4 PARADOX

Later in the book, we'll be talking more specifically about investing more time in the long-term growth of your ministry. And we'll even talk about how you can triple (yes, TRIPLE!) your time off.

But for now, practice making that subtle shift from being a Sunday-driven manager to an E4 Leader by embracing Parkinson's law. Dedicate the first 5 - 10% of your week to something other than this Sunday.

And remember...

If you focus on creating great Sundays, you might build an OK team eventually. But if you build an exceptional team, eventually, you can't help but have exceptional Sundays... every week.

Ready to shift to E4 Leadership?

If you want help making the shift to E4 Leadership, schedule an Exceptional Sunday Assessment. During this call, you and a coach will talk about…

- Where you want to lead your team…
- Where you're at right now…
- And what might be holding you back from reaching your goals.

Even if you decide it's not the right time or best fit to work with my team, you'll get tremendous amounts of clarity and value from this call.

There's no cost to you for this session, and you can schedule it here:

> https://www.worshipteamcoach.com/book-esa

Chapter 5

EXCEPTIONAL EVERY SUNDAY EXPLAINED

> *Welcome to Lake Wobegon, where all the women are strong, all the men are good-looking, and all the children are above average.*
> Garrison Keillor

If Every Sunday's Exceptional…

It's time to explain the title "Exceptional Every Sunday." And you've seen this phrase several times now: *build a team that can make every Sunday exceptional.*

So let's start with *Exceptional.*

If you're a 'language' person like me, it's time to acknowledge the linguistic elephant in the room:

If *every* Sunday is exceptional, then *no* Sunday is exceptional, right?

It's like Garrison Keillor's description of the town of Lake Wobegon: "all the children are above average."

EXCEPTIONAL EVERY SUNDAY EXPLAINED

This grammatical faux pas is intentional, and it's actually part of the process to lead consistently excellent Sundays. Here's how it works.

- As you're intentionally implementing what you learn in this book, or as we work together in one of our coaching programs, you'll start to have more excellent Sundays.
- Eventually, what was *exceptional* becomes *normal*. So this is your new standard. Hooray!
- From there, you work to grow to your *'next level of exceptional'* – whatever that is for your worship ministry.
- Over and over, what was once exceptional in your context now becomes typical and normal. And the good news is that you're measuring excellence against your own church and worship ministry – not what some other church or worship team defines it as.

And that's why we talk about being *exceptional every Sunday*.

It's not hyperbole!

It's a future reality that you'll create intentionally from your current reality as you implement the framework in this book.

(Read that sentence again.)

Changing the culture and building the kind of worship ministry you've always dreamed of leading requires reshaping reality.

That sounds trippy, but stay with me.

You can't be satisfied with where your team is at. (And if you're reading this book, I'm guessing you're not.) But you also have to fully embrace where your team is at right now and OWN IT.

Think about this – what do most leaders do when their worship teams aren't where they want them to be?

For example, they may have…

- Some solid musicians, but the music just sounds… *bleh*.
- Several team members who look like statues on the stage.
- A few Sunday "giggers." That is, the worship team is just a gig, and they don't attend church when they're not scheduled.
- Team members who get along, but there's no real friendship or deeper connections.
- A majority of spiritually lukewarm people with a few mature standouts.

So what do most worship leaders do with a team like that? Usually, one or more of these things:

They blame their team.

"My team members are the problem! If only they were better musicians, more expressive, more committed, yadda, yadda, yadda…"

They blame themselves.

"I must be a crappy leader. I can't get my team to do anything to grow." Then they fall into a downward spiral of self-doubt.

(By the way, 'owning' your team's current reality is NOT about blaming yourself and wallowing in self-pity.)

They look for a magic fix.

"If I could only go to the right conference. Or find the right training site. Or watch the right leadership video."

And that magic fix leads them in search of the next great improvement.

They fall into 'shiny tactic syndrome.'

"I need to teach my team the Nashville number systems. That'll help."

Or...

"I gotta start using tracks and loops."

Or...

"I need them to read 'The Heart of the Artist.'"

Now, none of these tactics are bad, but they're bandaids at best. Eventually, a leader will start to give up.

They become OK with being OK.

"It is what it is," becomes their motto.

Leading their worship team devolves into 'just getting by' each Sunday. Any long-term improvement is accidental at best.

So let me ask you, friend...

Does any of that resonate with you?

If it does, that's OK. We've all been there.

Any worship leader who's wanted to bring about real and lasting change to their worship team has gone through this death spiral of failed improvement efforts.

But let's break down what we're trying to improve in the simplest terms.

Ultimately, when it comes to building a team that can make every Sunday exceptional, you want 'future versions' of your team to…

- Look better…
- Sound better…
- Love better…

…than they currently are right now.

Let me break each of those down.

Look better is about being more expressive and engaging lead worshipers. On the production side, it's about creating an environment that encourages worship. That might include better lighting, lyric graphics, etc.

Sound better is a musical and technical thing. You want a band and vocal team who can create great music, and an audio engineer who can mix it well.

Love better is about how your team…

- loves and respects each other (and you),
- loves and serves the congregation,
- and how they worship God.

Now, raising the standards in any one of these three areas will be supremely difficult if you ignore the underlying team culture issues, which we'll get to later in this book.

EXCEPTIONAL EVERY SUNDAY EXPLAINED

But for now, let's keep walking through this phrase *Exceptional Every Sunday*.

Every Sunday??

> *"When you lead worship, don't shoot for a home run… just get a base hit every week."*
>
> Rick Muchow, founding worship pastor,
> Saddleback Church

This is an approximate quote from one of David Santistevan's earliest podcasts where he interviewed Rick.

When I heard it, I realized Rick had described the path of my ministry. For too many years, I swung for the fences every Sunday. I would…

- Schedule a full band at all costs.
- Run long rehearsals.
- Plan the latest and greatest songs.
- Cajole the congregation to get a response.
- Allow the quality of Sunday to determine my worth.

All the while my family, church, and team paid the price. It wasn't too great for my emotional and spiritual health either.

Over time, I shifted my mindset about Sunday excellence to a more sustainable pace – what Muchow described as a *base hit*.

If you aren't familiar with baseball, the "home run" is when one batter scores a run (what points are called in baseball) with one hit – typically hitting over the fence.

Home runs are exhilarating! They can turn the tide of a game. But they're rare compared to the number of strikeouts, walks, and singles over an entire season.

A base hit is fantastic, but there's no score. That is, not until you advance a runner to home.

And base hits don't make the highlight reels as often as home runs do. But I've heard my son's baseball coaches say it over and over through the years, "Base hits win ball games."

Rick's analogy is brilliantly simple. A string of solid Sundays over and over will advance a church and worship team forward over time.

Imagine what will grow a church of worshipers more...

The infrequent-to-rare 'home run' service with the perfect combination of the right songs, the right musicians, and a congregation that's in the mood to worship.

Or...

The 'base hit' service – a weekly worship gathering that's Biblically-grounded, musically solid, and has engaging leadership.

You'll hear people (the congregation, your senior pastor, other staff, your team, etc.) describe the 'home run' service as *transcendent... anointed... moving...* or *awe-inspiring*. But unfortunately, that's what they start to expect.

EXCEPTIONAL EVERY SUNDAY EXPLAINED

The 'home run' service unfairly becomes the unattainable standard for future Sundays.

The 'base hit' service won't initiate a rush of people to the platform afterward to tell you "worship was amazing today!!" But for the long-term spiritual formation of your church (and to quote *The Mandalorian*)...

This is the way.

This base hit mindset also won't kill you as you try to chase the unrealistic standards of a grand slam service.

And what's really critical here is this:

You can improve to a point where *every* service is consistently exceptional...

...no matter who's scheduled...

...and without burning out you or your team.

That's what this Exceptional Every Sunday Model will do. As you implement this framework and embrace E4 Leadership, not only will your team be consistently excellent, but you'll operate at a sustainable pace.

You might even feel a little guilty at first as your workload lightens and your pace relaxes. But don't. You weren't designed to be a one-person worship-production factory.

There will be no more "Sunday Crazy Cycle" for you. I mean that. You *can* build the kind of team you've always dreamed of leading.

But first, I need you to pinky-promise me one thing before you read any further:

"I _____ (state your name), do pinky-promise Jon that I will work to get off the never-ending Sunday treadmill and embrace the life-giving approach of E4 Leadership."

Did you do it?? Remember, that pinky-promise is binding.

Now, let's talk about how you build a worship ministry that makes every Sunday exceptional.

The Three Big Levers of Exceptional Sundays

I have a problem: as of this writing, I currently don't fit very well in roller coaster seats anymore.

It's embarrassing.

The last few years of dealing with the pandemic, middle age, and a thyroid issue have resulted in putting on enough weight to threaten my enjoyment at Cedar Point – the North American mecca for roller coaster enthusiasts.

Cedar Point is about an hour from where I live, and so we have season passes.

Guess what my motivation is to lose weight?

This seat:

It's from the ride, Steel Vengeance.[6]

One of Steel Vengeance's claim to fame is 27.2 seconds of "airtime" throughout the two and half minute ride. Airtime means literally that – going weightless with only the lap bar holding you in.

Now, the lap bar is supposed to rest on, well, my lap. But it stops at my stomach.

And so every time the coaster "gets air," I get the Heimlich maneuver.

The first time we rode it, my teenage daughter thought I was dying.

(I was.)

So now, my modest goal for next summer is to be able to secure it myself without the high school attendant having to push it into my belly with her foot.

---

[6] Photo credit: https://www.cedarpoint.com/blog/the-first-steel-vengeance-ride

(It's OK, you can laugh.)

Now, when it comes to losing weight there are essentially three big areas I've got to contend with:

- What I eat - *Diet*
- How I move - *Exercise*
- How I think - *Mindset*

I used to think diet and exercise were the only thing that mattered. But to have sustained weight loss – and keep it off – I've realized my mindset is huge.

So diet, exercise, and mindset are three "big levers" that will help me move this large rock called "Getting Healthy."

The more I can move each lever, the more I'll be able to enjoy the roller coasters next summer (and avoid a whole host of weight-related issues).

The levers (diet, exercise, mindset) move the rock. But what moves the levers?

When it comes to levers, you need force – something to act upon them.

So a healthy diet, exercise, and mindset are actually made up of hundreds of small but intentional choices.

- Planning my meals.
- Scheduling my exercise.
- Reviewing my goals.
- Tracking my meals.

EXCEPTIONAL EVERY SUNDAY EXPLAINED

- Avoiding late-night TV watching (which triggers me to want to eat).

And on and on and on… again, hundreds, probably thousands of intentional decisions to take positive action.

This doesn't sound very fun, does it? But there's a bright, shining moment for all this work that I'll tell you about in a minute.

But first, when we want to accomplish something big, we have to get small.

You've heard about the guy who stops drinking Mountain Dew and loses 30 pounds? (I've always hated that guy.)

The reality is for most of us, those 30 pounds won't come off with one big change. It's going to happen with a bunch of small changes and efforts.

By now you might be thinking, "Jon, did this suddenly become a weight loss book?"

Well, I could teach you to lose 180 pounds like I have. Unfortunately, it's just been the same 15 pounds over and over (and over!!). So let's just stick to worship ministry leadership.

Just like there are 3 Big Levers for getting my body healthy, there are 3 Big Levers to develop a worship ministry that produces exceptional Sundays consistently, week after week.

1. Experiential Worship Sets
2. Engaged Congregation
3. Essential Capacity Leadership

I'll only give you a quick summary on each one right now, because we'll be digging deeper into each one separately later.

Experiential Worship Sets

Each week, you need to plan, prepare, and lead worship gatherings that are more than just music sets. They want them to be powerful experiences – whatever that looks like in your context.

We'll talk more about how you can do that – at a sustainable pace without burning out you or your team. And, of course, without falling into the dangerous mindset of always needing to "top" last Sunday.

Engaged Congregation

You can plan and lead the most powerful worship sets. But if no one participates, it's just a pleasant concert.

We'll talk about what you need to do to get your congregation to not only *participate* in your gathered worship times, but also *anticipate* the gathering each week.

Essential Capacity Leadership

And finally, planning and leading weekly worship gatherings will take its toll on you. You also need the bandwidth to focus on more than just the upcoming Sundays. You need to be able to build a team for the long term.

That's why you need high capacity as a leader. And this isn't just about your time, but also...

- leadership skills,
- a growth mindset,
- and creating healthy margins, so you don't burn out.

EXCEPTIONAL EVERY SUNDAY EXPLAINED

Moving These Levers...

Again, just like weight loss, there is a combination of actions and tactics to move these "3 Big Levers" to grow your worship team and improve your Sundays.

Some actions are big with significant results. But most will be incremental. And it's those incremental movements that are the key.

Over time, you'll see that a culmination of smaller actions will cause ongoing change that eventually turns into... *MOMENTUM!*

Remember that bright spot I mentioned earlier?? This is it... *momentum!*

At first, all this work will feel like you're trying to push a boulder up a hill.

You are.

But with the right levers, you'll reach a place where it starts rolling downhill – in a good way. That is, your worship ministry will perform at a higher level with less effort from you.

That's where I was able to get to at my last church.

I eventually transitioned my team members, ministry structures, and leadership team to a place where I could maintain (and even improve) my ministry with only a few hours a week. I moved from being a full-time worship pastor to part-time status, so I could focus more time coaching other leaders.

After a certain amount of time and investment in intentional, incremental movements, you'll have...

- Systems & processes in place that get more done in less time.
- Other leaders who will help to carry the weight of the ministry.
- Team members who are "bought in" to a healthy culture of excellence – musically, spiritually, and relationally.

I want to say one last thing about these 3 Big Levers – Experiential Worship Sets, Engaged Congregation, and Essential Capacity Leadership.

These aren't just levers, but they're also the outcomes of embracing E4 Leadership and implementing the Exceptional Every Sunday model.

You'll have more time, more powerful worship gatherings, and a more engaged congregation when you implement this model.

Does this get you excited?? I hope so!

The Model

Are you ready to finally take a look at this model?

Heck yeah!! Let's go.

Warning: If I showed the entire model to you all at once, it could blow a large portion of your cranium right off. *Literally.* (And I mean that *figuratively*, thanks to the influence of my millennial friends.)

Now, you're perfectly capable of grasping this model. But seeing the whole thing without some explanation will just look like I'm inviting you into a MLM business opportunity.

EXCEPTIONAL EVERY SUNDAY EXPLAINED

Which I am. So if you get seven of your friends to implement the EES Model, and they each get seven of their friends, and so on, we'll all be Warren Buffet rich by next Tuesday.

You in??

OK, just kidding. It's not a pyramid scheme. I promise. But it is a triangle. And each of our 3 Big Levers / 3 Big Outcomes are a part of this…

```
            Essential
            Capacity

          EXCEPTIONAL
          EVERY SUNDAY

   Engaged              Experiential
   Congregation          Worship
```

As we progress through the remaining chapters of the book, I'll continue to build out this model by showing you…

- First, what's likely holding you back from building a team that's consistently exceptional every Sunday
- Second, how to *make the time* to implement this model.
- Third, how to cultivate the kind of culture you need to make this model work for you.

And finally, we'll talk about how to train and develop your team towards the new standards of excellence that this model requires.

In other words, it's about to get really practical. You ready??

Let's go!

Can we help you implement this?

If you want help implementing the Exceptional Every Sunday Model in your ministry, schedule an Exceptional Sunday Assessment. During this call, you and a coach will talk about...

- Where you want to lead your team...
- Where you're at right now...
- And what might be holding you back from reaching your goals.

Even if you decide it's not the right time or best fit to work with my team, you'll get tremendous amounts of clarity and value from this call.

There's no cost to you for this session, and you can schedule it here:

https://www.worshipteamcoach.com/book-esa

Chapter 6

BARRIERS TO EXCEPTIONAL SUNDAYS

"If you find a path with no obstacles, it probably doesn't lead anywhere."
Frank A. Clark

Now that we've defined the term *Exceptional Every Sunday* and determined the 3 Big Levers / 3 Big Outcomes, it's time to start talking about what's keeping worship leaders from making this a reality.

BARRIERS TO EXCEPTIONAL SUNDAYS

As you set out to create exceptional Sundays consistently through…

- Planning and leading powerful and *experiential worship sets*…
- Encouraging and cultivating a *culture of participation and engagement* in our congregation…
- And leveraging the *essential capacity* needed to invest in your ministry for long-term growth (without burning out)…

…you're going to encounter barrier after barrier after barrier.

It may feel like a bunch of individual obstacles…

- Attitude issues from a few team members.
- Team members not practicing.
- Not having enough time to work on implementing much-needed ministry structures.
- Last-minute call-offs.
- Team members who are non-responsive to scheduling requests.
- Pushback against your leadership.
- Another new song to learn. ("Thanks for that last-minute 'suggestion,' Mr. Senior Pastor.")
- People showing up late to rehearsal and sound checks.
- Focused work time getting interrupted by other staff members and long meetings.
- Vocalists who can sing (but are as expressive as tree bark).
- Instrumentalists who either spoon the music stand or stare at their fingers like they might fall off.

- Sound techs who just turn up their favorite instrument.
- Team members not showing up to training events and other team meetings.
- No one invests in their own skill development.
- Spiritually immature team members.
- Gig mentality musicians (they just show up to church when they're scheduled).

I could go on. And on. But every single one of these issues and obstacles are part of 3 Big Barriers to 3 Big Growth Areas.

So before we get to the big barriers, let's start with the positive and define the 3 Big Growth Areas:

Capacity

Capacity is the first big growth area. Not only do *you* need the essential capacity to lead your team, but your team members also need to be able to serve and minister without burning out.

So, when you use the wisdom of E4 Leadership to…

BARRIERS TO EXCEPTIONAL SUNDAYS

- implement efficient processes,
- empower the right people,
- and maintain a sustainable pace,

…you'll be able to build a team that makes every Sunday exceptional – no matter who's scheduled – *without* burning out you or your team members.

Culture

Culture is the second Big Growth Area. As I mentioned earlier, if the underlying culture issues don't change, any new initiatives or change efforts on your part will die a slow death.

```
              Essential
              Capacity
          EXCEPTIONAL
          EVERY SUNDAY
      Engaged         Experiential
    Congregation        Worship
```

Here's how culture fits in this model. When you're able to…

- create a clear and compelling vision…
- with firm expectations that move people toward that vision…
- and create ownership among your team to uphold those standards for themselves and others…

...you will build a ministry culture that values and pursues excellence – musically, relationally, and spiritually.

Capabilities

The third Big Growth Area, *Capabilities*, is about building your team to look, sound, and love at a continuingly higher and higher level of excellence.

```
        Essential
        Capacity
     EXCEPTIONAL
     EVERY SUNDAY
  Engaged        Experiential
  Congregation   Worship
```

When you're able to...

- Cultivate exceptional musicianship in individual people and as a team...
- Develop expressive lead worshipers whose private worship fuels their platform worship...
- Attract and onboard qualified team members who fit the desired team culture...

...you'll build a team that's consistently excellent every Sunday, no matter who's scheduled.

BARRIERS TO EXCEPTIONAL SUNDAYS

If not all of that made sense, don't worry. Those are just summaries for the 3 Big Growth Areas. I'll break down each of those in later chapters and give you actionable tactics to implement.

3 Big Barriers

So with each of the 3 Big Growth Areas comes 3 Big Barriers. Let's talk about each barrier and why it keeps worship leaders from leading consistently exceptional Sundays week after week.

The Capacity Barrier: Not Enough Time

There's no time for ministry development.

```
                  Essential
                  Capacity

             EXCEPTIONAL
             EVERY SUNDAY

        Engaged              Experiential
        Congregation         Worship
```
(Triangle with "No Time for Team Development" along the left side)

The demands of Sunday hinder the worship leader from investing in long-term ministry growth like leadership development, team member training, and implementing efficient systems and structures.

And because she doesn't develop additional leaders or run efficient systems, that requires an unsustainable pace to keep up.

Remember that *Sunday Crazy Cycle?* Yeah, this is that.

She's lacking the *Essential Capacity Leadership* to work ON her ministry because she spends all her time working IN it.[7]

The Culture Barrier: Not Enough Commitment

The team's not committed to high standards.

The team members fail to pursue high standards for one of two reasons.

1. Those standards aren't clear.
   Or
2. The standards are clear but not upheld. They're *stated* values, not *lived* values.

---

[7] This concept of working ON versus IN comes from Michael Gerber's book, *E-Myth Revisited*. In it, Gerber directs business owners to shift from being the one doing the work that the business requires to instead doing the work of designing a business that runs without the owner – developing leadership structures and processes that enable others to do the work. Sounds familiar, doesn't it? "Their responsibility is to equip God's people to do His work…"

BARRIERS TO EXCEPTIONAL SUNDAYS

While a leader may have some on the team who take ownership of excellence, many do not. It's part of that 'mixed bag' of skill and maturity we discussed earlier.

What propagates the growth of this barrier is the previous Big Barrier. Because of Sunday's demands, the leader has little capacity to...

- Determine a clear direction (vision).
- Build systems and create expectations that align people's behavior with the vision.
- Grow leaders and committed team members who hold each other accountable to clear standards.

While the leader might be able to plan a powerful, experiential journey of worship, the team cannot execute at the level of excellence required.

And the frustrating thing for the leader is this: most of the team is content with that.

They're OK with being OK.

The Capacity Barrier: Not Enough Depth
The team doesn't look or sound good enough.

```
                    Essential
                    Capacity
         EXCEPTIONAL
         EVERY SUNDAY
       Engaged          Experiential
     Congregation         Worship
   Team Doesn't Look or Sound Good Enough
```
(Triangle diagram with edges labeled: "No Time for Team Development", "Team's Not Committed to Standards")

That statement, "*the team doesn't look or sound good enough,*" may sound harsh (and even a little crass) given that this is, well, *church* and all.

But this statement is just the unvarnished truth that we worship leaders will admit only when we're around other worship leaders who get it.

And, if you remember, we talked about how these words – *look better, sound better, love better* – are just a shorthand for building a team that can make every Sunday exceptional.

So let's look at each of these deficits.

The team doesn't look good…

They lack engagement. In a future chapter, we will discuss what it takes to improve the expressiveness and engagement of your team members. (And maybe you, too.)

Also, the tech areas – lyric graphics, lighting, video, etc. – can contribute to a substandard "look" of the service. (But I'm not touching the tech stuff. That's a different book I'm fully unqualified to write.)

BARRIERS TO EXCEPTIONAL SUNDAYS

The team doesn't sound good…

They lack musicianship – individually and as a team. The overall sound, of course, also hinges on the house mix. (Which, again, I'm not touching tech stuff.)

Now, the idea of "doesn't look or sound good enough" is *relative*. What one worship leader calls 'subpar' musicianship and platform presence, another worship leader would be willing to commit a crime to obtain that quality.

So, I'm not defining what "*look good*" or "*sound good*" actually is. You already know that in your context, and you can see that many of your team members aren't reaching their potential level of excellence.

But what about *loving good…*?[8]

As I mentioned above, we want to build a team that looks better, sounds better, and loves better. And we're going to talk in a later chapter about where *loving better* fits into this Exceptional Every Sunday Model.

Overcoming the 3 Big Barriers

Now that I've defined the 3 Big Barriers, I'll invest the following three parts of the book to help you overcome those. But, before that, let's look at what's on the far side of those barriers.

---

[8] OK, it should be "loving well." But just cut me some slack, Captain Grammar.

Lack of Time

To bust through the first Big Barrier, *No Time for Team Development*, we're working to give the leader enough time to meet the high demands of Sunday AND have time to...

- Develop their team.
- Implement healthy, productive systems.
- Take healthy time off for family, rest, and restoration.

Simply put, the *leader has enough time.*

Team Doesn't Look or Sound Good Enough

Lack of Standards

To bust through the second Big Barrier, *Team's Not Committed to Standards*, we're working to create a team culture committed to excellence – musically, spiritually, and relationally.

BARRIERS TO EXCEPTIONAL SUNDAYS

Lack of Quality

To bust through the third Big Barrier, *Team Doesn't Look or Sound Good Enough*, we'll be working to build a team that's consistently exceptional *every* Sunday.

Easy-peasy-lemon-squeezy, right?

I wish.

Remember, this model is a map – a picture of the journey. But it doesn't take the journey for us. Breaking through those three barriers will require intentional leadership and effort.

But we've already talked about the alternative – staying stuck in the Sunday-after-Sunday grind. I assume you don't want that since you've read this far. So just know that each chapter from here to the end is full of practical stuff to show you how to…

- Free up more time…
- Build a culture of excellence, and…
- Grow a team that's consistently exceptional every Sunday.

Again, I want to help you get results on your own. But as you have some success implementing this yourself, just know that my team and I can help you make this ministry model a reality at a pace that would be almost impossible on your own.

So let's get you some results in the first Big Growth Area, *Leadership Capacity*.

BARRIERS TO EXCEPTIONAL SUNDAYS

Want to move at a faster pace than DIY?

If you want help implementing this leadership model into your ministry – at a pace that would be impossible on your own – schedule an Exceptional Sunday Assessment.

During this call, you and a coach will talk about…

- What you would do if you and your team had the capacity, culture, and capabilities you can only dream about now…
- Where you're at right now with your time, culture, and team capabilities…
- And what might be holding you back from reaching your goals.

Even if you decide it's not the right time or best fit to work with my team, you'll get tremendous amounts of clarity and value from this call.

There's no cost to you for this session, and you can schedule it here:

https://www.worshipteamcoach.com/book-esa

Part 3

CAPACITY

How to Have Enough Time & Energy to Transform Your Team

Chapter 7

ESSENTIAL CAPACITY LEADERSHIP

Fatigue makes cowards of us all.
Vince Lombardi

When *Get To* Devolves Into *Have To*

The thought hit me as I was turning onto Hanley Road. Our two services were finally over, and the church building was in my rearview mirror.

"I have to do this all over again next week."

During the five years previous to this moment, I had turned around a highly dysfunctional team and finally won over a big contingency of the congregation who liked my predecessor better. (I described this in more detail in Chapter 2.)

Also, during some of that time, I had to appease a hands-on, micromanaging senior pastor and deal with a governing board member on my team who wanted my job. He was resentful that the church hired me instead of him.

ESSENTIAL CAPACITY LEADERSHIP

Then came transforming two campuses into two independent churches and renovating an old warehouse for our permanent church home.

And, again, all that during that time, I was leading Sunday after Sunday after Sunday.

Ugh.

Earlier in ministry, my thought was always,

"I GET to do this all again next week!"

But that day, driving home on Hanley Road, it was a moment of despair:

"I HAVE to do this all over again next week!"

I had lost the *essential capacity* to do my job as a worship ministry leader.

If you skipped over some chapters and started reading here, *Essential Capacity Leadership* is one of the 3 Big Levers to create consistently exceptional Sundays.

It's about having the bandwidth to be an effective, healthy leader. And like other leadership concepts, it's easier to describe it by examining what happens when you *don't* have it.

So I want to show you the three big problem areas – deficits – when you're running on low capacity.

3 Big *Essential Capacity* Deficits

1. Your Time Deficit

Essential capacity goes far beyond having enough hours and minutes to get your work done.

One massive issue? Too many leaders don't take enough time off and work too many hours. Guess what suffers:

- Your marriage and family.
- Friendships outside of work (the ones that truly matter).
- YOU!

(We'll talk more about the emotional, spiritual, and physical toll overworking takes on you in a moment. But for now, just know all this stuff is interconnected.)

Essential capacity as a worship ministry leader also means you're able to invest in more than just THIS Sunday.

When you get sucked into a singular focus on the upcoming worship services, you become a Sunday-driven manager. As a result, you put the long-term work of building your team on the back burner.

Does any of that resonate with your experience? Maybe this doesn't. But these other deficits might.

2. Your Emotional & Spiritual Deficit

If you are stuck in a "Sunday-driven management" cycle and not taking the time off you need, you'll hit the proverbial wall sooner or later.

ESSENTIAL CAPACITY LEADERSHIP

And before you do, you will experience emotional and spiritual fatigue, which *always* affects you physically.

This eventually leads to burnout if there's no change in your approach to ministry leadership.

Here are some symptoms…

- You feel like you can't get off the weekly crazy cycle of Sunday after Sunday.
- You feel like you can't take enough time off to get the rest and restoration you need.
- You'll start to lose the joy you had. Leading your team and leading worship becomes a *have-to*, not a *get-to*.

I'm seriously happy for you if you've never felt any of this and can't imagine feeling it.

But just so you know, I never imagined feeling that level of despair.

Until I did.

And these two deficits, *not enough time* and *emotional / spiritual fatigue,* compound to cause another deficit.

3. Your Leadership Deficit

When you don't have the essential capacity for leadership, you go into survival mode.

This means you only focus on the *urgent* work – getting ready for Sunday. You end up neglecting the non-urgent (but critical) work of growing your team for the long term, as well as bettering yourself.

When you're in this low-capacity state…

- ***You avoid the real issues on your team.*** Commitment, attitude issues, people not practicing, spiritual immaturity – it's all too much to deal with.
- ***You avoid critical soul work.*** When you get into the crazy cycle, you don't have time or energy to invest in your own growth and self care. And eventually, all this leads to…
- ***You avoid trying to improve Sundays.*** You get stuck in a *status quo* mindset when you don't have essential capacity. *You become OK with being just OK.*

All this is part of the survival mode we fall into during the early stages of burnout.

If you've ever felt this way or are currently feeling this way, I want you to hear me:

This is normal and you're not alone. Unfortunately, nobody prepares leaders for the high cost of church ministry.

And…

I've got your back. My team and I are here for you if you're feeling the effects of the Sunday grind.

That's one of the biggest reasons I'm writing this book. Yes, I want you to experience the fabulous reality of leading a team that can make every Sunday exceptional.

But more than that, I want you to lead and love your team, church, and (most importantly) your family from a place of wholeness.

ESSENTIAL CAPACITY LEADERSHIP

So... What Now?

I've painted a bleak enough picture of what happens when we don't have essential capacity.

So now, how do we fix this??

Let me give you three easy tips.

...
...
...

Yeah, there are no easy tips to fix this.

In fact, if you had the urge to punch me in the throat when I offered three easy tips, I don't blame you one bit.

Recovering your essential capacity requires a shift in leadership mindset. The remedy to the fatigue of Sunday-driven management is E4 Leadership. There is freedom and fullness when we embrace and live out the ancient leadership wisdom of Ephesians 4:11-12.

Over the next three chapters, I will give you three specific objectives that will help you gain, grow, or recover your essential capacity for leadership.

These are *not* quick tips.

They're outcomes you work towards. But for each outcome, I'll give you practical steps and tactics you can apply.

Let's preview them now to see how they fit on the Exceptional Every Sunday Model.

1. Simplify Sunday Planning

In the long term, simplifying your Sunday planning is about delivering high-quality worship gatherings week after week without burning out.

In the short term, it's about freeing up one, two, or even three hours each week to reinvest into your ministry. Then, you can invest in the next objective with those extra hours.

2. Build Supportive Structures

Supportive structures are the processes, ministry systems, and leadership frameworks that allow you to accomplish ministry work. In Chapter 9, we'll cover the specific structures and systems you must have in your worship ministry.

As you build these supportive structures in the right way, you'll accomplish more in less time and have more leaders, allowing you to reach the next objective.

3. Triple Your Time Off

Yes. You read that right: *TRIPLE!*

To grow your essential capacity, you need to take enough time off. In Chapter 10, I'll show you how to strategically 3x your time off so you can be at your best – first for your family and then for the church.

Here's how those outcomes fit into our model.

ESSENTIAL CAPACITY LEADERSHIP

Team's Consistently Exceptional EVERY Sunday

Again, each of the following three chapters goes in-depth on those three objectives to help you make progress on your own.

But, maybe you're at a place where...

- You know you want more leadership capacity and you want to get there quicker than a DIY approach...
- You're teachable and open to coaching and mentoring...
- You're willing to put the time and effort into growing as a leader...
- You're open to exploring something that will require you or your church to invest financially in your leadership...

...if so, let's talk.

Even if you decide it's not the right time or best fit to work with my team, you'll get tremendous amounts of clarity and value from this call.

There's no cost to you for this session, and you can schedule it here:

https://www.worshipteamcoach.com/book-esa

Chapter 8

SIMPLIFY SUNDAY PLANNING

Productivity is never an accident. It is always the result of a commitment to excellence, intelligent planning, and focused effort.
Paul J. Meyer

By now, I hope it's clear that making every Sunday exceptional is far more than the songs you pick and the band you schedule for next weekend.

Ongoing, long-term Sunday excellence is a *by-product* of the culture you create, not the sets you plan.

(Read that sentence again.)

But the setlists, service flow, and scheduling all still matter. Big time! Let's face it; if you neglect the work of 'this Sunday' to build your team or implement systems, you could find your job at risk. Or, at least a few eyebrows raised at the next board meeting.

Because of that risk, I want to show you how to plan your Sundays in a way that allows you to get more done in less time.

SIMPLIFY SUNDAY PLANNING

I also want to help you deliver a worship service that meets (or exceeds) your current standards while investing two, three, or even four hours *fewer* than you usually do.

When you learn to do this consistently, you'll have more capacity to work ON your ministry versus IN your ministry.[9] That is to say, you'll have more time to invest in building your team for the long term.

Before I give you some practical ways to simplify your Sunday planning, let's first talk about *what* we're trying to accomplish and *why*.

It may seem counterintuitive, but one of the keys to making every Sunday exceptional is simplifying your worship planning.

It's not about having 'simple' worship services. I'm not trying to dictate the style, feel, and/or complexity level of your service. But I want to help you simplify your *planning* so you can get more done in less time. In other words, *productivity*.

It might seem "unspiritual" to purposefully truncate the time you invest into Sunday.

But it's *not*.

Worship leaders too often hide behind the twin excuses of "*I'm a creative*" and *"I'm Spirit-led"* to rationalize their disorganization and time-wasting tactics.

Good productivity practices don't stop you from being creative *or* Spirit-led. Instead, productivity skills allow you to accomplish more in a shorter time frame.

---

[9] I mentioned this concept of ON vs. IN briefly in Chapter 6.

Like any artist, your creativity needs boundaries. The painter has the dimensions of a canvas, the potter's wheel is only so big, and the sculptor can only remove pieces from the chunk of granite – not add them.

Your time limitation is a healthy boundary to your creativity. A compressed time frame gives you more focus to complete the work. In a moment, we'll talk about why this is, and I'll give you some examples.

But first, let's talk about the second excuse for wasting time: being "Spirit-led."

The Holy Spirit can lead us as we plan using an efficient process as easily as He can through a prolonged, open-ended, free-flowing state.

Too many leaders who use the 'led by the Spirit' excuse are just rationalizing their disorganization. They don't want to submit to an intentionally time-limiting, organized process.

You might still struggle to reconcile productivity with worship planning. In that case, I'd just ask you to suspend judgment for a few minutes while we look at the three critical objectives of productivity. You'll see it's *not* just about saving time.

The Three Critical Objectives of Productivity

1. Stewardship

When applied to worship planning, the heart of healthy productivity is *stewardship*.

Your time is valuable – to you, your family, and your church.

SIMPLIFY SUNDAY PLANNING

If you're a vocational worship leader, simplifying your Sunday planning helps you be a good steward of your church's finances. When you reduce your Sunday planning time and achieve the same, or better, quality of worship service in less time, that's good stewardship.

If the church *doesn't* pay you, it's even more important to steward your limited bandwidth and not overgive of yourself. Otherwise, you're stealing time from your family and your own well-being.

There's a more subtle and important aspect of stewardship than your church's finances.

The real heartbeat of stewardship is this:

- Treating something like it's your own…
- While never forgetting Whose it is…
- Always working to give it back better than you found it.

If you spend all or most of your work week (whether that's 40 hours or 4 hours) focused only on "this Sunday," you'll neglect the long-term growth of your team.

Think about the *Parable of the Three Servants* (aka *Parable of the Talents*) in Matthew 25. The Third Servant is only focused on *right now*. He tells himself this story: "I don't want to lose my Master's money."

So, he *buries* it.

First Servant and Second Servant tell themselves a different story and invest what they have.

They *multiply* it.

EXCEPTIONAL EVERY SUNDAY

"But that's too risky," Third Servant thinks. And, yes, at any given moment, the Third Servant is reasonably certain he still possesses what he was given.

That's like the worship leader who only focuses on 'this Sunday' with no regard for the long-term growth of his team. He values the security of a solid Sunday 'this week' more highly than the potential but uncertain future growth of his ministry.

He's a Sunday-driven manager. And Sunday-driven managers *play it safe*.

Like First Servant and Second Servant with their bags of silver, the E4 Leader risks some of the safety of a 'status quo quality' Sunday to invest in the long-term growth of her worship ministry. But in the long run, giving up the security of a 'safe Sunday' pays big dividends in future excellence.

It's the E4 Paradox.

Remember that?

If you focus on creating great Sundays, you might build an OK team eventually. But if you work to build an exceptional team, eventually, you can't help but have exceptional Sundays… every week.

When your 'primary investment' is developing your team, you'll eventually have exceptional Sundays every week, which require far less time than you're investing now.[10]

---

[10] 'Primary investment' doesn't mean that you'll spend the *most* time here. You'll still spend more time on Sunday (at first). But it's your 'primary investment' because of a mindset shift. We'll talk more about this later.

SIMPLIFY SUNDAY PLANNING

And simplifying your Sunday planning is the first practical step toward making time to grow your team, leaders, and ministry structures.

2. Sustainable Excellence

You run an organization with a *weekly deliverable* – the Sunday worship service. As I mentioned in an earlier chapter, Sunday-driven managers chase excellence.

Whether they're pressuring themselves or they allow others (senior pastor, congregation, etc.) to push them towards an unsustainable level of excellence, there's a problem.

If you've felt that pressure, you know deep down you can't maintain unrealistic standards week after week and hope to survive, let alone thrive. It *will* catch up with you eventually.

Undefined excellence is an ever-moving horizon line. No matter how much progress you make, it will always be off in the distance.

That's why in an earlier chapter we talked so much about the "next level of exceptional." What was once a "beyond your capacity" level of excellence can eventually become your typical Sunday standard.

In other words, what was once *extraordinary* became *ordinary*. And I mean *ordinary* in the best possible way. I stopped chasing home run services and committed to planning solid services sustainably – in a way that created space for me to invest in other things besides Sunday.

When you first start embracing this Exceptional Every Sunday Model, sustainable excellence begins with being more efficient with your Sunday planning.

But that doesn't mean neglecting the *craft* of Sunday planning – the songs you pick, the people you schedule together, the service flow you create, etc. All that is still incredibly important. You need to learn to plan with *both* excellence and efficiency.

We'll discuss specific tactics to plan your Sundays more efficiently in a moment. But first, let's talk about the third objective of healthy productivity.

3. Delegation

Delegation isn't just an objective, a goal we want to get to. Delegation is also the *ultimate* productivity tactic. If done correctly, you're getting multiple times the work done because you're not doing it all.

You might think, "Jon, have you ever delegated anything before? It's NOT simple. It makes life more complicated."

You're right, *partially*. Delegation is not simple, and it is complicated and messy. For a while.

But it's a leadership skill you must get comfortable with if you're going to build a team that can make every Sunday exceptional. The most effective tactic to free up your time is to have someone else do the work for you.

Remember Ephesians 4:11-12? We can't "equip the people to do the work of ministry" and have multiple people sharing leadership *without* delegation.

If you want to pursue the way of E4 Leadership, delegation has to become a routine part of your ministry. I don't have space in this book to teach you how to delegate effectively. But let me get you started on the journey towards it.

SIMPLIFY SUNDAY PLANNING

When you apply better productivity practices to planning, you'll create a *repeatable*, efficient process. Repeatable first by you, later by others.

Because of that repeatable process, you'll be able to teach someone how to do what you do.

First through *information* (you tell them how to do it).

Then through *imitation* (they watch and copy how you do it).

Eventually, they'll find better or more efficient ways of doing the work, which is *innovation*.

That process of *information* and *imitation* ensures the delegatee gets the job done right. The process of innovation creates a culture of ownership and continual improvement. You can't manufacture that when you're the only one leading.

> **7 Steps to Delegate Anything**
>
> As we work with leaders to build a team that's exceptional every Sunday, we teach them *System Mastery*, the seven-step, proprietary approach to transform any ministry system or process to a place where it...
>
> - Moves their team towards your vision.
> - Gets the results they want with high efficiency.
> - Can be easily delegated to another leader or team member.
>
> Schedule an Exceptional Sunday Assessment to learn more about how we can help you delegate at a high level.
>
> https://www.worshipteamcoach.com/book-esa

Again, I don't have the space here to teach delegation in depth. But when you start creating an efficient, repeatable process to plan your services, you'll create fantastic services in less time. And, you'll pave the way towards multiplying yourself through delegation.

To jumpstart you, here are five practical tactics to begin speeding up your worship planning.

5 Tactics to Cut Your Planning Time

1. Limited Song Rotation

One of the best ways to simplify your Sunday planning is to limit the number of songs in your active rotation list.

SIMPLIFY SUNDAY PLANNING

This is actually part of a major system area in your worship ministry: how you rotate and manage your songs. We'll talk more about this ministry system in a later chapter, so let me just give you the five-word summary:

Rotate fewer songs more often.

When you do this, it's easier to plan music since you aren't sifting through a monster catalog of 284 songs. Also, there are some massive benefits for your team and congregation. But we'll get to those in a later chapter.

(If you want to learn more about this concept, check out my book, *The SongCycle: How to Simplify Planning and Re-Engage Your Congregation*. Buy it from Amazon.com or go to www.worshipteamcoach.com/songcycle.)

2. Batch Processing

Batch processing is a "time management technique that includes grouping similar tasks together and setting aside a time to complete them all or work on them until a predetermined point of progress."[11]

As you apply batch processing to worship planning, you'll discover that it takes less time to schedule *four Sundays at one time* than it does to schedule *four Sundays at four different times*.

Not only does it save you time, but it helps keep you focused. That improves your final product. Also, it allows you to predict better how much time something takes.

The biggest advantage of batch processing is that it keeps you from 'context switching.'

---

[11] Mary Clare Novak, GoSkills.com

For instance, when you're in the mode of selecting songs, don't stop to determine the transitions between your songs or scriptures you might use. That requires a different focus and pattern of thought.

Now, I don't have time here to teach all the nuances and ways you can apply batch processing to your Sunday planning.

But as you're planning your upcoming Sundays, begin to take note of everything you do to schedule people, plan sets, prepare for rehearsals, etc. As you review that list, ask yourself, *what activities could I group together from multiple Sundays to apply batch processing?*

3. Automation

Worship leaders don't often think about automation, unless it's figuring out how to run their lights and lyrics through Ableton. Otherwise, automation's just for manufacturing and robots, right?

But let me give you four ways you can automate your worship planning, as well as other administrative tasks in your ministry.

Templates

Templates are something you create once and use over and over.

Your worship service is a great example of this. You're likely following some sort of pattern for the flow of worship elements. Whether it was printed on a bulletin 38 years ago and hasn't changed since, or it's just a pattern you've settled into (until your lead pastor gets a wild hair to change it), you've got a template for your worship service.

This is nothing new.

Patterns for sacred Christian gatherings have been used since the second century, maybe earlier. The human brain craves predictability and patterns. But besides benefitting your congregation, an intentional template jumpstarts your planning.

I created templates in the PCO Services App for two kinds of services we had – our regular service and our monthly communion service. It saved me from thinking through all the steps, elements, and time frames. They were already in the template. All I needed to do was choose the right template and customize it for that particular week.

We don't have space to talk about all the opportunities here. But you can apply templates to dozens of things in your ministry. Simply notice when you're doing a task that you've done before. Is there a way to create a template to speed up the work and avoid recreating (literally) the initial work every time?

Routines

Routines are a way to 'automate' yourself. Set specific times to complete predictable and recurring tasks in your ministry.

I had a particular day of the month when I planned music sets for the following month (batch processing). And I also had a specific time I scheduled musicians every month.

Here's a weekly example. I blocked time every Monday afternoon to get the service order as complete as possible. Since I already had chosen the songs, I used that time to add scriptures, segues, special service elements, band notes, etc., so I was ready to talk about it at our Tuesday staff meeting.

Delegation

Delegation is the ultimate automation – someone else is doing the task. Since we already discussed delegation, I won't go into it here other than to give you a starting point:

If someone else can do a task that takes you more than five minutes, look for a way to delegate it. Even if you have to invest several hours over a few weeks to offload it effectively, it's worth it. It won't feel like it at first, but the math for delegation (done well) always wins out.

4. Timed Work Sessions

Always use a timer when working on tasks that can easily take too much time. This tactic leverages Parkinson's law: *Work expands to fill the time allowed for it.*

List all the activities and tasks that you do regularly that will balloon out if you're not careful. Here are a few to get your list going:

- searching for new songs
- working on arrangements
- writing rehearsal notes
- planning sets / services
- meetings, etc.

For all these activities, set a timer (or have a 'hard stop' time in the case of meetings) to help keep you focused. And make sure you eliminate as much outside distraction as possible – put your phone on 'do not disturb,' shut your office door, put on noise-canceling headphones, etc.

Then, each time you approach those tasks or activities again, shorten the time you give yourself to complete them. Eventually, you find a sweet spot for the minimum, optimal time you need.

5. Recycled Sets

Yep, you have my permission: recycle your past services and sets. You've done the work. Why not reuse them?

Now, if I'm honest, I didn't do this for a long time. It felt unspiritual and lazy.

Why did I feel that way? Because in a season of poor self-management, I got desperately behind on planning. So, I pulled out a service I had planned six months prior and just changed the date.

As a band-aid to bad time management, recycling your sets *is* lazy.

But as an intentional tool for simplifying your Sunday planning, I learned to do it with integrity. Here's how:

- First, I didn't allow myself to "phone it in." I considered if a previously planned set of music fit with the upcoming Sunday.
- Second, more often than not, I opted to use partial sets and song pairings that worked well together rather than entire sets.
- Third, I often modified and freshened up these recycle sets. Sometimes I changed out songs. Other times I just swapped out elements like segues or scripture readings.
- Fourth, I gave myself permission to recycle a previously planned set 'as is' in hectic seasons, provided I did the first step.

Where to Invest Your Freed Up Time?

I want to reiterate that simplifying your Sunday planning isn't about just getting more done in less time.

In the long term, it's about delivering a high-quality worship gathering week after week without burning out.

In the short term, it's about freeing up one, two, even four hours each week to reinvest into your ministry. That is, you can spend that extra time working on systems, structures, and processes that will help you build a team that can make every Sunday exceptional.

In the following chapter, we'll move on to the next leadership outcome and look at which systems, structures, and processes you need to work on.

SIMPLIFY SUNDAY PLANNING

Free up 3 hours!

It's not uncommon for worship leaders to free up 3 - 4 hours a week (or more) when they start working with us.

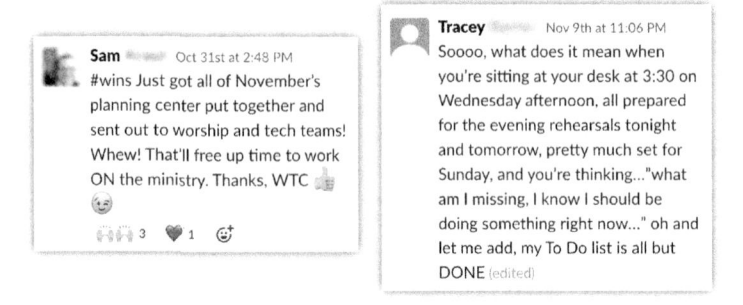

Sam Oct 31st at 2:48 PM
#wins Just got all of November's planning center put together and sent out to worship and tech teams! Whew! That'll free up time to work ON the ministry. Thanks, WTC 😊
3 ❤ 1

Tracey Nov 9th at 11:06 PM
Soooo, what does it mean when you're sitting at your desk at 3:30 on Wednesday afternoon, all prepared for the evening rehearsals tonight and tomorrow, pretty much set for Sunday, and you're thinking..."what am I missing, I know I should be doing something right now..." oh and let me add, my To Do list is all but DONE (edited)

Would you like help freeing up Sunday planning time so you can reinvest it into the long-term growth of your team? Schedule an Exceptional Sunday Assessment.

During this call, you and a coach will talk about how you can become the kind of leader who has the time to work ON your ministry – rather than always stuck working IN your ministry.

https://www.worshipteamcoach.com/book-esa

Chapter 9

BUILD SUPPORTIVE STRUCTURES

"80% of your problems are not people problems; they are systems problems, because systems create behaviors."
Andy Stanley

Can I tell you some really bad news?

You will never have enough time to do everything your worship ministry requires.

But that's actually *good* news. Leaders who try to control every part of their worship ministry face…

> Increasing frustration.
>> Unhealthy conflict.
>>> Inevitable burnout.

They frustrate themselves, their team members, their senior pastors, and, most of all, their families.

However, when you implement the Exceptional Every Sunday model into your worship ministry, you'll build leadership structures and processes that *decrease* your active involvement in all but the most crucial areas of your ministry.

BUILD SUPPORTIVE STRUCTURES

By the way, that's a *good* thing.

Remember, we're working to create more time for you to invest in your team. In the last chapter, we talked about simplifying your Sunday planning to free up time while still delivering a high quality worship service.

In this chapter, I'll show you the supportive structures you need to build, so you can…

- Lead a complex ministry (with minimal time investment).
- Empower others to lead (without micromanaging or redoing their work).
- Ensure your team bears a healthy amount of responsibility (without burning them out).

As you implement these supportive structures, you'll multiply – many times over – your essential capacity to build a team that can make every Sunday exceptional.

At the heart of these supportive structures are eight ultra-critical systems.

What Are Systems?

Systems, simply put, are how you or your team get something done.

For example, how you and your team prepare musically for Sunday is a system. *Preparation* is a series of complex processes that combine…

- Events and activities
  (Personal practice, rehearsals, warm-up, soundchecks, etc.)…

- Expectations for the team members
  (Learn the songs, show up at rehearsal on time, etc.)...,
- Responsibilities of the leader
  (Plan songs far enough in advance, post the charts and recordings of the songs, run an efficient rehearsal, etc.).

Here's the good (and bad) news:

You already have a system for everything.

The way you...

- plan music
- schedule your team
- run rehearsals
- distribute music
- qualify new people for your team

...those are all *systems*.

They might be accidental and unintentional systems, but they're still "the process by which you get something done." And the sobering truth is this:

The systems you have in place <u>right now</u> are perfectly designed to get what you're getting <u>right now</u>.

If you have a team member who backs out at the last minute or even no-shows, that's related to a system problem. Aren't there heart issues at play here? Sure, but the uncommitted behavior keeps happening because your system allows it to keep happening.

BUILD SUPPORTIVE STRUCTURES

Andy Stanley, pastor and organizational leadership guru, says that almost every 'people' problem is actually a 'system' problem.[12]

Why?

Because systems create behavior – good or bad. And that's *good* news.

As leaders, we can't change someone's attitude or heart. But we can change the systems that allow an attitude or heart issue to continue unchecked. If you have a good system, you will, over time, change your team's behavior and create a healthier culture.

And just so you know, this "system stuff" isn't all just organizational leadership tactics.

God is a God of Systems

Think about us traveling around the sun – we're a part of a solar *system*. Think about your breathing – it requires your respiratory *system*. Creation is filled with *systems*.

But God also used systems to help organize and lead his people.

In Exodus 18, Jethro is the first organizational consultant who helps his son-in-law, Moses, create a system of delegated leadership. We see it again in Acts 6. The apostles appointed the seven deacons to take care of people, so they could stay focused on the ministry of the Word.

We also see that Paul lays out the essential components of a leadership system to build the church in Ephesians 4. He tells us that Jesus has

---

[12] *Systems: Liberating Your Organization,* a Catalyst message by Andy Stanley. This is an older talk, but it's absolute gold. If you can find this talk online, watch it. Twice!

given us interdependent leadership gifts that work together to build up the people to do the work of ministry.

Systems are crucial to the work of ministry. And every worship ministry has Eight Essential Systems that will enable you to manage and grow your ministry effectively.

Your Eight Essential Ministry Systems

Now, there are dozens of processes working inside of your ministry. But most of those fall under the Eight Essential Systems.

Again, each of these Eight Essential Systems contains dozens of connected processes, structures, steps, and tasks. None of them exist in a silo. Instead, each Essential System is interconnected and interdependent on the others.

But to help worship leaders build out the critical structures and processes, it's useful to categorize these major ministry systems.

The first way we group them is by recognizing that some systems are primarily Sunday-focused, while others are mainly team and ministry-focused. There are four in each one.

The Sunday-Focused Systems are…

1. Service/Set Planning
2. Song Rotation and Management
3. Preparation
4. Scheduling

BUILD SUPPORTIVE STRUCTURES

The Ministry/Team-Focused Systems are…

1. New Team Member Qualification Process
2. Team Member Development
3. Leadership Development
4. Communication

Let's define each one briefly:

Service/Set Planning: The process for selecting music, planning segues, and creating a flow to the sets and/or services.

Song Rotation and Management: The process of managing a healthy song rotation that promotes active participation by the church.

Preparation: The processes and expectations to enable the team to be musically ready for worship services.

Scheduling: The process of creating your team schedule (rotation/roster), and the expectations for individual team members to respond appropriately to scheduling requests.

New Team Member Qualification and Onboarding: The process of attracting, qualifying, inviting, and onboarding new team members into the ministry.[13]

Team Member Development: Your discipling and development process to teach people the skills, knowledge, and character they need to be successful team members.

---

[13] I'll also just refer to this as the "audition process" or "onboarding" simply as a shorthand because *New Team Member Qualification and Onboarding* is a mouthful.

Leadership Development: Your process for identifying, training, and deploying leaders in (and from) your ministry.

Communication: The processes for communicating vision, values, and expectations with your team. It also includes the logistical communication for running the ministry and even the interpersonal communication you foster among the team.

(Yeah, your Communication System is a huge deal.)

More, Please?

We don't have the space to dive into each of these Eight Essential Systems here. But throughout this book, we will go into some detail about several of these systems. In fact, we already have. For example, Chapter 8 touched on three major systems: Scheduling, Set/Service Planning, and Song Rotation and Management.

But as you're shaping your ministry around this Exceptional Every Sunday Model, you will want to learn more about how to design each system area to be efficient, healthy, and aligned with your vision.

Here are two options:

First, we have on-demand courses called the RENOV8 Workshop Series. These uber-practical workshops give you step-by-step instructions to create or renovate each of these eight system areas. In most of the RENOV8 Workshops, we even provide done-for-you, customizable content to make implementation even easier.

The RENOV8 Workshops are your DIY (do-it-yourself) option. You can learn more about them here:

www.worshipteamcoach.com/8systems

BUILD SUPPORTIVE STRUCTURES

Second, you can apply to be a part of our private coaching group. It's our DWY (done-with-you) option.

While we still use the RENOV8 Workshops with our coaching clients, we take a more hands-on and guided approach to help them create and implement changes in their ministry systems.

If you'd like to learn more about the private coaching group, schedule an Exceptional Sunday Assessment here:

https://www.worshipteamcoach.com/book-esa

System Stages

All your ministry systems are currently in one of four different stages. It helps to know which stage each of your systems are in, so you know which one to prioritize and work on first.

Here are the four different stages.

1. Create

In this stage, you need to intentionally develop the system.

OK, I know what I said earlier: you already have a system in each of these eight areas. But in this stage, they're happening unintentionally or haphazardly. They haven't been designed for the desired outcome, efficiency, or sustainability.

So essentially, you have no *intentional* system – you're creating it from scratch or close to it.

2. Renovate

When a system is in this stage, it needs significant reworking or upgrading. It's lacking in several ways:

- It's not aligned with your vision (more on this later).
- You don't have a clear step-by-step workflow or process. The process is different every time you execute it.
- The expectations and responsibilities of the team aren't fully defined or clearly communicated.

An intentionally built system will sometimes return to this stage when the ministry experiences significant change (good or bad). For example...

- During a leadership or personnel turnover.
- Because of substantial growth – people, campuses, etc.
- When hiring an assistant / associate, etc. who will take on much of the work of a system.

But even if they're intentionally built, solid-running systems still need changes and updates. And that's the next stage.

3. Innovate

In this stage, you need to *optimize* the system for clarity, efficiency, and momentum. It's already a good system, but it needs to go that last 10-20% towards high efficiency.

So why did I use the word *innovate* – other than it rhymes with both *Renovate* and *Create*?

The simple definition of innovation is to "make changes in anything established."

BUILD SUPPORTIVE STRUCTURES

At certain growth junctures, your systems will need something fresh or new. It's recognizing that leadership adage: "What got you here won't get you there."

To grow, expand, and multiply, the system has to be adapted to reach those new outcomes. The good news is you rarely have to institute a full renovation or overhaul of the system. But you will have to make changes to something that's working well.

4. Delegate

At this stage, the system needs to be *codified* so another leader or assistant can take over leadership or management of this area.

If you try to delegate significant parts of a ministry area before any of these previous stages, it will fail.

The Delegation Stage is a continuation of the Innovation Stage where the leader asks, "What part of the system requires me?" She then seeks to remove herself from that.

Delegation isn't just about preparing the system to be delegated; it's about preparing *the person* who will lead or manage this area.

If full delegation isn't feasible yet, this phase is also about automation, templatization, and documentation (mapping out the workflow).

Those activities will…

- Prepare this ministry area to be delegated eventually.
- Help the leader prepare to let go of this part of the ministry.
- Reduce the work and attention this system requires while still allowing it to run efficiently.

When you have someone who *can* take over an area of your ministry, it's tempting to rush the Delegation Stage. But if you don't prepare the system to be delegated well, it will frustrate you and the delegatee. On the flip side, you also don't want to drag your feet and hold onto something too long.

So let me give you a brief checklist that will help you know if a ministry system, or parts of the system, are ready to be given to someone else.

- You're crystal clear on the outcome and have documented this process's objectives.
- You've documented the workflow for each step well enough that someone without working knowledge of the process could figure it out.
- You've identified *who* is responsible for *what* at each step in the process.
- You've determined clear deadlines and/or time frames for each step of the process.
- You've followed the workflow steps yourself to make sure they're accurate.
- You've documented all the assets a person needs to do this job – links, apps, login credentials / passwords, online tools, equipment, key / access card to a specific room or office, etc.

If you've done this work, your chances of delegating well are much higher. But still be prepared for a bumpy ride as your replacement learns to drive.

BUILD SUPPORTIVE STRUCTURES

You'll be tempted to grab the wheel and start steering again. But you have to learn to walk the line between allowing them a few bumps and scrapes and letting them crash and burn.

Your Systems' Stages

Take a few moments and quickly determine which stage each of your Eight Essential Systems is in. In the space below, put a C, R, I, or D (for Create, Renovate, Innovate, or Delegate) next to each system.

- _____ Service/Set Planning
- _____ Song Rotation and Management
- _____ Preparation
- _____ Scheduling
- _____ New Team Member Qualification/Onboarding
- _____ Team Member Development
- _____ Leadership Development
- _____ Communication

One of the traps leaders fall into is mistakenly putting a ministry system in the Innovate Stage rather than in the Renovate Stage. That system area might be running reasonably well. But there's one key characteristic of a healthy ministry system that we haven't discussed yet: *vision alignment.*

If a system isn't fully aligned with your vision, it needs a deeper renovation.

Vision Alignment: Efficiency & Excellence Aren't Enough

Each of your system areas need to be aligned with the vision of where you want to lead your team, your congregation, and even yourself. Why?

Systems produce outcomes. So you need to ensure those outcomes move you closer to your vision.

And more importantly...

Systems shape behavior. You need to be 100% sure that your system requires the kind of behavior you want from your team.

Let me give you an example.

Jess, a worship pastor, has a vision for a team who shows up on time to rehearsal with their music learned. But she's constantly frustrated that several of her team members are still learning their parts at rehearsal. And quite a few are showing up late.

But Jess is unknowingly part of the problem.

First, she waits until the last person arrives before she starts rehearsal. Second, she will stop rehearsal to allow a team member to figure out a part he should have learned at home.

The rehearsal is part of the system of preparation. And right now, Jess is running it in a way that's not aligned with her desired future. Her 'system' is allowing – heck, even *encouraging* – people to show up late with their music only partially learned. So her current expectations won't produce her desired outcomes.

BUILD SUPPORTIVE STRUCTURES

Expectations are a mission-critical part of every ministry system. That means that every single expectation inside a system needs to align with the vision. If not, that system won't produce results consistent with the vision.

Later in the book, we'll discuss vision-driven expectations more deeply.

But right now, let me give you an easy way to determine which systems (and which parts of those systems) aren't fully aligned with your vision and why.

Start with the problem.

First, observe. Whatever problem, issue, or shortcoming you see in your worship ministry, write it down. (You could probably write a dozen things or more right now.)

Second, identify which system, or systems, affect this issue.

Third, determine which parts of the system allow, enable, or even encourage the issue, behavior, or attitude.

Fourth, ask yourself (or better yet, ask a group of trusted leaders and/or team members):

What needs to change about this system so it produces the behavior, attitude, or outcome that aligns with our vision?

You'll likely have a daunting list of changes for multiple ministry systems. But let me give you one parting piece of hard-earned wisdom:

Tackle only one system at a time.

If you try to fix multiple ministry systems at one time, you will...

- Frustrate yourself (too much work).
- Frustrate your team (too many changes).
- Dilute your efforts (too many plates spinning).

So instead, focus on ONE system area per quarter. (That's three months – Quarter 1 is January to March, Quarter 2 is April to June, etc.)[14]

And as you work on renovating each of your Eight Essential Systems, you'll be building the leadership structures and ministry processes that will…

- Free up your time…
- Equip and deploy leaders…
- And build a team that can make every Sunday exceptional.

Overload?

Now, I know talking about assessing eight different systems and trying to figure out where to start can feel really overwhelming.

It can be a system overload. (Sorry, bad pun.)

Because of this, when worship leaders join our private coaching group, I help them cut through the clutter to assess their systems immediately.

After that, we triage those systems to determine which ones need the most work and which will produce the *most results* if renovated and aligned properly.

So if you'd like help dealing with system overload, let's talk.

---

[14] Crud. I think I just *mansplained* what "quarters of the year" are. Sorry.

BUILD SUPPORTIVE STRUCTURES

Help to demystify your systems...

Most worship ministries are a tangled mess of half-developed systems. It can get overwhelming and confusing as you consider where to focus and what to do.

If you want help assessing your systems and prioritizing which one to focus on first, schedule an Exceptional Sunday Assessment. During this call, you and a coach will talk about…

- Where you want to lead your team in the next six to eighteen months…
- Which systems will be crucial to get you there…
- And what might be holding you back from reaching your goals.

Even if you decide it's not the right time or best fit to work with my team, you'll get tremendous amounts of clarity and value from this call.

There's no cost to you for this session, and you can schedule it here:

> https://www.worshipteamcoach.com/book-esa

Chapter 10

TRIPLE YOUR TIME OFF

> *"If you don't take a Sabbath, something is wrong. You're doing too much, you're being too much in charge."*
> Eugene H. Peterson

> *"Let me teach you, because I am humble and gentle at heart, and you will find rest for your souls. The burden I give you is light."*
> Jesus

Triple my time off??!?

This idea is just nutty-bananas for a lot of worship leaders.

For some, they're thinking, "How am I supposed to take a bunch of Sundays off when I'm the only leader?!"

For others who take their allotted vacations and even get time off for conferences are thinking, "Wait, you want me to take MORE time off?"

But hang with me for a second.

If you're going to lead exceptional Sundays every week, you *cannot* be the only person leading every Sunday. It's not healthy for you, your family, your team, or your church.

Lone ranger worship leaders...

- create a cult of personality...
- fail to develop other leaders...
- frustrate their family...

...and eventually burn out.

You need to be emotionally healthy.

Nothing will kill the consistent quality of Sundays more than a governing board-enforced sabbatical of the main worship leader.

To steadily increase your team's excellence and grow it for the long term, you have to develop a team of worship leaders...

...and get yourself *off* the platform!

Now, I don't mean you should suddenly disappear, shirk your responsibilities, or take three weeks of vacation multiple times a year.

What I mean by 'triple your time off' is that you need to take at least three types of Sundays off.

3 Types of Time Off

1. "Away" Sundays

This is when you're absent from the Sunday service because you're on vacation, going to a conference, on a weekend getaway with your spouse, etc. It's that typical time off that most worship leaders think of.

But the next two are even more critical than this.

2. "Off-Platform" Sundays

This is when you're not away, but you're also not leading. You can actually worship with your family. (Whoa… your spouse probably wouldn't know what to do with you sitting there!)

These "Sundays off" are critical not just for your emotional health but for…

- your family (they miss you)…
- your team (you need to model healthy time off the platform for them, too)…
- your leaders (they need more chances to grow and not feel like they're just substitute leaders).

At times, these 'Off-Platform Sundays' will allow you to spend time in the production booth encouraging and learning from your techs.

If your church runs multiple services, take advantage of that. For example, worship with your family during one service, and hang with your techs during the next.

And bring donuts. Your techs will appreciate it.

Finally, the third 'Sunday Off' might be something you only do a few times a year, but it's crucial for your emotional and spiritual health.

3. "Sabbath" Sundays

This is when you don't go to church… *anywhere*.

TRIPLE YOUR TIME OFF

Leading worship is your job (whether get paid for it or not). Even if you go to another church, you know you'll slip into note-taking and comparison mode, right? That's not real rest.

Imagine if you were able to do this:

> Sleep in on a Sunday.
> Get up and enjoy your morning coffee.
> Stay in your PJs till lunch.
> Go on a hike.

Whatever is personally restorative for you, do it.

> Just
>   don't
>   go
>   to
>   church!

(I promise you'll be able to find God somewhere else on Sunday morning other than a church building.)

A Side Note

Those of us who have grown up in the church can have a complicated relationship with Sunday worship attendance. For some, taking this 'Sabbath' Sunday can feel sinful. Or at least guilt-inducing.

But that's exactly why you need it.

I know I'm opening up a big can of worms, but it's critical. And not enough people are telling worship pastors and church leaders this. You *need* a few Sundays a year where no one expects ANYTHING of you.

God will NOT be angry. Or disappointed.

Some people in your church might be disappointed or even angry. But remember, Jesus got flack for this. And what did he say to them?

"The Sabbath was made for man, not man for the Sabbath." (Mark 2:27)

So... How?

Now the big question is HOW? How do I take more time off?

Before I tell, let me deal with some common objections I hear.

I push the worship leaders I coach to take at least six Sundays off the platform a year, even more – preferably once a month. And we talk about how those Sundays need to be a mixture of the three different kinds of time off.

But one of the common objections I get from them is this:

It's more work to take time off than it is just to stay here and lead!

I get it. I know several leaders who only take vacations from Sunday afternoon to Saturday, so they can be there on Sunday to lead.

I'm tempted to ask these leaders, "Have you ever heard the term *codependency*?"

But, again, I get it. The benefit from the time off rarely offsets the amount of work required to take a Sunday off.

That's why I encourage worship leaders to take at least two Sundays off in a row when going on vacation. The amount of work it takes to prepare two Sundays won't feel that much more than one Sunday. But you'll have a longer time to rest and recuperate.

Eventually, as you build the right systems and a team of leaders, taking off a Sunday is far less hassle. And hint, you'll even get to a place where it becomes relatively easy.

The other big objection to taking more (or any) Sundays off is this:

"No one can lead besides me!"

I get this objection, too. I've been on staff in smaller churches. Usually, it's not that *no one* can lead. It's that the *someone* who *can* lead isn't as good or well-received.

If that's your church, tell them to get over themselves.

OK, so maybe don't use those *exact* words. But impress on your church leadership how important it is for you AND the church that you get a break from the platform. Heck, share this chapter with them.

The bottom line is this:

Your emotional and spiritual health is worth a few Sundays of diminished quality.

Now, if there truly is no one at your church who can lead other than you, ask your church to bring in a guest worship leader a few times a year.

The cost will depend on your church's standards. A guest worship leader could range from as little as $100 and up to $1000 or more.

If you're in a small church, you should be able to find someone adequate to lead at the far lower end of that scale. But please, pay this person! The worker deserves their wages. (1 Timothy 5:18)

However much your church pays, it's worth the investment to help you stay healthy.

Now, long-term, the solution isn't guest worship leaders. Instead, it's building your own team of leaders – which we'll get to in later chapters.

Easing In More Time Off

When you start moving towards more time off – preferably monthly – you won't just have to deal with one 'who' – as in, who's leading for me. But there are other 'who's' affected by this.

You'll need to ask, *How will my...*

- *Senior pastor or leadership board receive this idea?*
- *Congregation react to different worship leaders besides me?*
- *Team feel about someone else leading – or a guest team replacing us all a few times a year?*

If you're a "53 out of 52 weeks a year" worship leader, you probably won't be able to make that leap right away to monthly time off – or even every other month. Nor should you!

The transition to acceptance by your church, team, and leadership will likely take longer.

Instead, aim for once a quarter. And then, after nine to twelve months of that, work to increase the frequency slowly. After a while, your church will acclimate to other leaders, and you'll be able to speed up the pace at which you add Sundays off to your schedule.

TRIPLE YOUR TIME OFF

While you'll likely have a few loud complainers, you'll probably be surprised how quickly your church embraces multiple worship leaders.

And, as you're able to train and unleash those worship leaders to help you deliver exceptional Sundays, you'll be able to take even more Sundays off. Which means…

- You're more excited and refreshed for the Sundays you're on.
- You've got better emotional health.
- Your family gets more of you.
- Your team and leaders learn to step up without you.
- Your church learns to enjoy multiple worship leaders.

If that doesn't sound fabulous to a worship leader who is currently leading almost every Sunday, chances are he's an unhealthy person who derives his self-worth from being the ONE – *the Dude* – THE worship leader.[15]

But if you've read this far, I'm guessing you're NOT that person. You're more than ready to find a way to triple your time off. So keep reading because the rest of this book will help you move in that direction.

---

[15] There's a female version of this leader, too. Men aren't the only ones whose egos prevent them from taking time off. I just happen to see it more often with the male variety.

Can we help you 3x your time off?

If you want help building a healthy time off into the regular rhythms of your ministry, schedule an Exceptional Sunday Assessment.

During this call, you and a coach will talk about…

- Where you want to move with time off and leadership development …
- Where you're at right now with leadership and time management…
- And what might be holding you back from reaching your goals.

Even if you decide it's not the right time or best fit to work with my team, you'll get tremendous amounts of clarity and value from this call.

There's no cost to you for this session, and you can schedule it here:

https://www.worshipteamcoach.com/book-esa

Part 4

CULTURE

How to Create a Culture that Pursues Excellence

Chapter 11

CREATING CULTURE (OR, HOW TO NAIL JELLO TO A WALL)

> *People like us do things like this.*
> Seth Godin

If you're going to build a team that can...

- make every Sunday exceptional,
- no matter who's scheduled,
- and without burning out you or your team...

...you're going to have to address the issue of culture.

Why?

Change won't stick without a culture shift.

Any improvements you make will be incremental at best (and may not even last) unless you transform the underlying culture issues.

CREATING CULTURE (OR, HOW TO NAIL JELLO TO A WALL)

Unfortunately, attempting to write a short chapter on *how to create a healthy culture* is like Peter Jackson trying to make *The Lord of the Rings* in just one film. (Harvey Weinstein told him he could only make one movie. Peter prevailed, thankfully.)

For the non-nerds who don't concern themselves with hobbits, let me translate what I'm saying:

Culture is a massive and complex topic.

Not only is it complex, but no one thing shapes culture. Because of this, changing it can feel overwhelming because so many different elements create and sustain a team's culture.

Look at this definition of organizational culture from a business consulting firm:

Culture is the expectations, experiences, philosophy, as well as the values that guide member behavior. It also includes the organization's vision, values, norms, systems, symbols, language, assumptions, beliefs, and habits.[16]

Now that you have the definition of culture, go ahead and start changing all this in your worship ministry…

>   *Expectations*
>   *Experiences*
>   *Philosophy*
>   *Vision*
>   *Values*
>   *Norms*
>   *Systems*

---

[16] Gothomculture.com https://gothamculture.com/what-is-organizational-culture-definition/

Symbols
Language
Assumptions
Beliefs

Oh, and don't forget *Habits*.

So, yeah, remember what I said about overwhelming? Changing the culture of a team is like trying to nail green Jello to the wall.

(I guess it doesn't have to be green. I just happen to like green Jello.)

Now, at some point, if you want to grow an exceptional worship ministry, you certainly should confront each of those elements on that list.

But let me give you some *hope* and *handles*.

Hope & Three Handles

First, the *hope*:

You can do this!

You can transform the culture of your worship ministry and build the kind of worship ministry you've always dreamed of leading.

I'm going to get you started in these next few chapters. And if you want me and my team to help transform your culture faster and with less guesswork, let's schedule a time to talk.

Schedule a time to talk to a coach here:

https://www.worshipteamcoach.com/book-esa

CREATING CULTURE (OR, HOW TO NAIL JELLO TO A WALL)

Next, three *handles*.

Before we can get a grip on a big, squishy concept like culture, we need to start small and simple and work out from there.

I love Seth Godin's simple explanation of culture:

"People like us do things like this."

Take a second to think about this: What *things* do you want your *people like us* – your worship team – to *do?*

Let me give you a jumpstart and summarize the broad strokes of a desired culture:

"I want us to be able to lead consistently exceptional Sundays every week, no matter who's scheduled, and without burning out."

To do that, worship leaders need to get their teams to *look better*, *sound better*, and *love better:*

Look Better

- Be confident on the platform.
- Worship with genuine expression.
- Engage the congregation.

Sound Better

- Prepare well.
- Play/sing tight and together.
- Create a dynamic, musical journey of worship.

Love Better

- Love God on and off the platform.
- Love each other and assume the best about each other when there's conflict.
- Love the congregation.

As you flesh out what each of those "look better, sound better, love better" aspirations mean for you, you'll get an even more tangible picture of what you want.

And do you know what you're actually doing?

You're clarifying a compelling vision. (That's the first handle!)

Will it be a pretty statement you can stencil on your green room wall?

Heck no! It's far better than that.

You're painting a picture of the desired future. And once you've started that, you can start the next thing:

Create vision-driven expectations. (That's the second handle!)

All your policies, rules, and guidelines will now serve a purpose beyond "behavior management." Expectations show your team *what to do* to reach the vision.

Once you get crystal clear on what you expect from your team, you'll...

CREATING CULTURE (OR, HOW TO NAIL JELLO TO A WALL)

Uphold loving standards. (The third handle!)

So how do you uphold loving standards?

- Design your systems to reinforce the desired behavior and attitudes.
- Grow supportive leaders who help you uphold those standards.
- Equip your team to see that these expectations help them look better, sound better, and love better – and why all that matters.

Then, as your team starts to live out these expectations, their attitudes and behaviors will shift. And when their attitudes and behaviors begin to shift, do you know what happens?

You've changed the culture.

So let me review these three "handles" to help you get a grip on your team culture:

- Clarify Compelling Vision
- Create Vision-Driven Expectations
- Uphold Loving Standards

And here's how it fits into our Exceptional Every Sunday model…

Diagram

```
                    Essential
                    Capacity
1. Simplify Sunday Planning          1. Clarify Compelling Vision(s)
2. Build Supportive Structures       2. Set Vision Driven Expectations
3. Triple Your Time Off              3. Uphold Loving Standards

        Leader Has Enough Time  /  Committed to Culture of Excellence
        No Time for Team Development / Team's Not Committed to Standards

              EXCEPTIONAL
              EVERY SUNDAY

        Engaged                    Experiential
        Congregation               Worship

        Team Doesn't Look or Sound Good Enough
```

Team's Consistently Exceptional EVERY Sunday

In the following three chapters, we're going to look at each of these "handles" to help you get a grip on your team culture.

Again, you CAN do this! The next chapter will get you started.

Chapter 12

CLARIFY COMPELLING VISION

As your leader it's my job to provide a vision. But frankly, I'm not seeing anything.
Dilbert's Boss

What has 35 words, sounds really profound, and no one remembers it?

Your vision statement.

Ba-da-CHING!

You're right, I should've gone into comedy. Or been a senior pastor. (Because too many of them *think* they're comedians. Am I right or am I right?)

Despite the droves of forgettable and (nearly meaningless) vision statements out there, vision *is* critical. There's no way to change your worship team's culture without it.

In the last chapter, I quickly told you how vision helps shape culture:

1. You create a clear picture of where you want to go – the desired future.

CLARIFY COMPELLING VISION

2. Next, you create expectations for the behavior that drives people (including yourself) toward that vision.
3. Then, you hold people (including yourself) accountable to those expectations.

Also, in Chapter 9, I talked about how you need to align your systems to produce outcomes congruent with your vision. And we'll talk more about vision-driven expectations and vision-aligned systems later in the chapter.

But first, let's make sure we're all on the same page with this word *vision*.

Vision often gets interchanged with *mission* and even *purpose*. So here's how I'm defining *vision* versus *mission* or *purpose:*

Vision is a clear, tangible, descriptive portrayal of the desired future. It's a 'pre-depiction' of...

- The actions people will take.
- The attitudes people will have.
- And the outcomes those attitudes and actions will result in.

If you think *mission* is a better word for this concept, it's OK. You're just wrong. (Ha! Kidding! We'll agree to disagree.)

Mission is more of a description of an overarching purpose or general direction. Or, if it does have to do with a future accomplishment, it's much broader and less specific.

A common mission statement you see in church is, "To know Christ and make Him known."

Or, "Love God, Love People, Serve the World."

Or, "Save Money, Live Better"

Wait, that's Walmart. But you get the drift.

Mission tends to be big, overarching, and not terribly specific. And that's what a mission or purpose statement is supposed to do: give an easy-to-reference "North Star" to point the desired direction.

But unlike *mission* and *purpose,* vision is the full-color, seven-panel brochure of the five-star family resort you're vacationing at next summer. [17]

(It's the brochure you pull out to show your kids and then threaten to leave them at home with their Great-Aunt Kay-Kay if they don't stop bickering.)

A working vision isn't a fancy slogan or statement you memorialize on the wall. It's something you live out.

And while good leaders try to distill their vision into memorable statements, the desired future is too big to print on a Successories® poster (under a trio of hot air balloons lifting off at sunset, no less).

And you can have a pithy statement – but it won't be your full vision. That statement is a rallying cry, reinforcement, and reminder. I'll give you some examples later in the chapter.

For now, let's go a little deeper into what vision is, why it's important, and what it accomplishes.

---

[17] Because you've tripled your time off!

CLARIFY COMPELLING VISION

What Vision Is

The kind of vision that will help bring about the desired future and reshape your culture for the better is this – clearly determining…

- Where you're going.
- Why you're going there.
- What it looks like when you arrive.

If you can articulate those three points, you'll have a clear vision.

Someone might be thinking, "But WHY is vision so important? Isn't it just rah-rah, let's-get-charged-up future-babble? I'd rather stay in the present and get real stuff done."

Without a plan or process to achieve it, that person is right – *vision is worthless*.

But the right vision with the right plan to get there is absolutely critical to changing your culture.

Why Vision Is Critical

Let me give you seven reasons why vision is a key to helping unlock culture change.

1. Vision defines the WHY.

People need to understand the reasons why you're proposing this change. Without a compelling 'why', most people will have difficulty buying into a vision that calls for significant change.[18]

---

[18] Rather than elaborate further, you just need to watch Simon Sinek's "Start With Why" Ted Talk. I think 11 trillion people have already viewed it, so you've probably seen it by now. But if you haven't, just Google "Simon Sinek" and you'll find it.

2. Vision clarifies direction.

Now, vision isn't only about a future destination. It's also the direction we're oriented toward in our vision-aimed present. We're not there, yet, but we're moving in the right direction.

One of the most common things I hear from frustrated worship team members about their leader is, "There's no clear direction." (That, and, "She keeps *Good, Good Father* on a ridiculously high rotation!" But that's a different issue.)

A clear, compelling vision helps your team see where you're leading them.

3. Vision creates metrics.

If there's no way to measure your vision, it's too vague. Now, I get it; our worship-leading metrics aren't as cut and dried as the nickels and noses the senior pastor is counting.

But a good vision includes tangible, achievable, and measurable outcomes. And even more important than that, you can also measure the activities and efforts that help move your team toward the vision.

4. Vision limits decisions.

It helps you know what to say yes or no to. For example, the worship leader from the church down the street calls and says, "Hey, we're doing a community night of worship. We'd love to have you and some of your team join us." That's a good thing.

But, is it the *best* thing? If it doesn't get you closer to your vision, you might need to say no.

CLARIFY COMPELLING VISION

5. Vision tightens focus.

When you're working towards a real, achievable, and desired future, it's easier to stay the course. A compelling vision will help you stay focused on the path, projects, and processes that will help you transform your current reality into that future.

6. Vision anchors expectations.

Good vision connects and grounds expectations (policies, rules, guidelines, etc.) with a purpose. When people see the purpose for the policies, they'll be more apt to adhere to them.

We'll be going into this idea in more detail soon.

7. Vision strengthens fortitude.

Without a clear, purposeful reason why you're chasing this future reality, it will be too easy to quit when things get tough. A clear and compelling vision will help keep you motivated by reminding you (and your team) of the bigger picture and the better future.

How Vision Shapes Culture

Let's now look at how clarifying a compelling vision will help bring about a worship ministry culture that pursues excellence – musically, spiritually, and relationally.

This may sound antithetical to what I've been saying all along, but…

Vision doesn't shape the culture.

Plenty of worship leaders have a fantastic vision for where they want to lead their team, but they're still stuck in the status quo, churning out mediocrity Sunday after Sunday after Sunday.

The real power of vision is that it helps you shape the stuff that shapes the culture:

- Systems
- Expectations
- Leadership
- Influence
- Language

Let's look at each one briefly.

Systems

Remember what I said in Chapter 9, *"Systems shape behaviors."* That's why every last system and process in your ministry needs to align with your vision. If it's not, your ministry is working against you.

This is so critical that I'm going to talk more in-depth about vision-aligned systems later in the chapter.

Expectations

Expectations are how a worship team makes progress toward the vision. These are so critical that we'll spend an entire chapter on *vision-driven expectations*.

Leadership

As you develop leaders and a leadership team, these people must have commitment to and ownership of the vision. Otherwise, they will dilute it or distract you from your vision. Or worse, they'll lead your team directly towards a counter-vision.

CLARIFY COMPELLING VISION

Influence

If your vision is going to result in true culture change, you will need to influence almost everyone on your team to get on board with it.

If you've never tried this kind of wholesale culture change, let me explain what it's like:

> *Imagine closing a car door on your head.*
> *Repeatedly.*

So yes, influencing your entire team to change is painful and might result in your death. But hey, we're leaders; it's what we signed up for.

To create buy-in and ownership for your culture-changing vision among your team and leaders, you have to leverage influence. The movement of influence in any group or organization can be seen on the Diffusion of Innovation bell curve:[19]

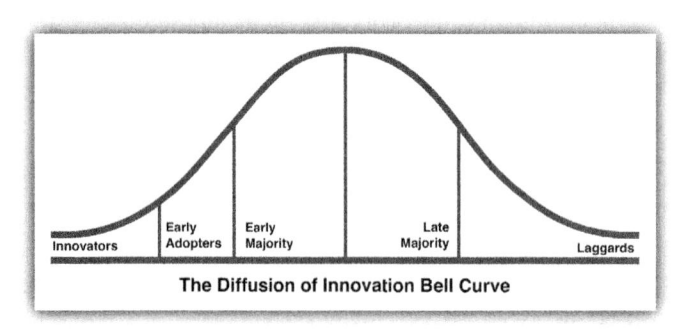

The Diffusion of Innovation Bell Curve

Innovators | Early Adopters | Early Majority | Late Majority | Laggards

Your influence as a leader will convince *some* of your team to commit to your vision. Those will be your 'innovators' and 'early adopters.'

---

[19] Diffusion of Innovation (DOI) Theory was developed by E.M. Rogers in 1962.

But, you'll have a large portion of your team who won't be convinced or fully onboard. And that group will buy into your vision at different rates.

The 'early majority' will come on board fairly quickly. After that, the late majority will see your "new-fangled ideas" are working and get with the program.

Then there are the 'laggards.'

After seeing overwhelming evidence, they may conclude that this culture shift is inevitable and reluctantly get on board. But, they may not. So, you get to be in the unenviable position of either uninviting them to the team or enduring their dissension.

Now, why do I tell you all this? Because culture change happens person by person. And each person influences another. You and the early adopters on your team will have almost no influence on those to the far right of the bell curve – the 'late majority' and 'laggards.'

Influence spreads from left to right on the bell curve. The early adopters will influence the early majority. The early majority will most directly persuade the late majority. And when the late majority buy in, they're your best shot at getting your laggards on board.

Language

How we talk about something and the words we use shape not only our culture, but our minds.

There's a fascinating TED Talk from Lera Boroditsky, a cognitive scientist, who shared a story about an Aboriginal community in Australia, the Kuuk Thaayorre people, who use cardinal directions (north, south, east, west) instead of "left" or "right."

Borodtisky stated they say things like, "Oh, there's an ant on your southwest leg." Or, "Move your cup to the north-northeast a little bit."

Because of this unique part of their language and culture, this group has the ability to orient themselves better than scientists thought possible for humans.[20]

Let me give you an example of language shaping culture in the church ministry world.

Instead of calling our stage a *stage*, I pushed our staff and team to call it a *platform*. A *stage* is a place people perform. And while there are plenty of musical performance elements in our Sunday worship gathering, I wanted to change the notion about our role.

My senior pastor wasn't sure we needed to make the intentional shift in our nomenclature. But I explained to him that a high percentage of the worship team – artists, musicians, creatives, etc. – are performance-oriented people prone to find their worth from accolades and applause.

So, instead of performing for the audience on a *stage*, we had a *platform* from which we encouraged and led the congregation in worship.

Over time, we intentionally started using the word *platform*. I would look for opportunities to talk about the difference between a performer's *stage* and lead worshiper's *platform*.

---

[20] How Language Shapes Culture - Lera Boroditsky - TedWomen 2017 https://www.ted.com/talks/lera_boroditsky_how_language_shapes_the_way_we_think?language=en

While not nearly as profound as knowing which way 'southeast' is from any given location at any given moment, the shift from *stage* to *platform* made a subtle difference. It reinforced the idea that we were on that platform to fulfill a dual-role purpose: *worship God and serve the congregation.*

Later in the book, I'll give an example of how language helped shape our culture of preparation significantly.

What If I'm NOT a Visionary?

What do you do when you're not a visionary leader?

So many worship leaders I talk to say, "Jon, I'm just not a visionary leader," or "I can't come up with a vision for my team."

I'm here to tell any leader that they can determine a vision for their team and lead with vision.

Let me revisit the definition of vision:

It's your *desired future*.

- It's not a pretty statement on the wall that no one can remember.
- It doesn't have to have originated from some prophetic event.
- It's not a purpose statement of why you or your team exists.

It's simple clarity about…

- where you want to go,
- why you're going there,

CLARIFY COMPELLING VISION

- and what it looks like when you arrive.

Because of this, "leading with vision" isn't something only persuasive, natural-born dominant personality types can do.

If you've struggled with having vision or leading with vision, take courage. You can do it, and I want to show you how.

But first…

There *is* a type of person who tends to gravitate towards vision. It's the future-oriented person.

That's me.

I've lived most of my life one month, one year, five years, (or more) into the future.

It's what Yoda said about Luke to Obi Wan in the Dagobah swamp…

"This one a long time have I watched. All his life has he looked away, to the future, to the horizon. Never his mind on where he was, what he was doing."

Ding ding ding!! That's me! (Unfortunately, I don't have the ability to levitate droids. Sorry.)

Future-thinking is so natural to me that it was a shock to learn that not everyone thought that way. It always felt so good and natural to dream, scheme, and plot my future.

I found out there are some who are focused naturally on the present. (Seriously??)

And some tend to gravitate toward the past. (Why??? It's done!)

But I soon learned that present-oriented people could help me stay grounded and focused while I moved toward my vision. And those who thought more about the past could help me avoid mistakes that others made. That is when I listened to them.

I think the past/present orientations are at the heart of why so many worship leaders think they aren't visionary leaders.

They're not *NOT* visionary leaders.

They're just *not* naturally future-oriented. But they can easily overcome that with some guidance.

That's why our Exceptional Sunday Assessment is so helpful to leaders. A coach can help you articulate where you want your team to be in the next 12 - 18 months. And we help you flesh out what that looks like with a three-part plan to get there.

On the flip side, there are those leaders who are so future-oriented they have idealistic dreams coming out of the wazoo. But, they don't have a clue of how to get from *here* to *there*.

The Exceptional Sunday Assessment also helps that person. If that's you, the coach will help you rein in all your future ideas so you can determine the most essential parts of your vision to work on. And even more critically, your coach will help you create a plan to start making real progress toward your vision.

Go to this page and sign up: https://www.worshipteamcoach.com/book-esa

Vision is Messy

Let me wrap this chapter by reviewing a few key ideas to remember.

CLARIFY COMPELLING VISION

Vision is NOT a fancy statement you put in a frame and hang on the wall.

It's about defining where you're going, why you're going there, and what it looks like when you arrive.

You don't have to be a charismatic visionary to lead with vision.

If you are a charismatic visionary with future ideas dripping out of every pore of your body, you need to always remember the next key idea.

Vision without a plan to achieve it is just a daydream.

Too many 'visionary' leaders frustrate the people around them because they don't ever create (or find someone else to create) a plan to get them from *here* to *there*.

Now, speaking of getting from here to there, let's get real about implementing vision. There are three words I want you to remember as you start to implement your vision.

1. Overwhelm.

Your plan to reach your vision will be overwhelming. If it doesn't freak you out or overwhelm you a little, it's probably not a big enough vision.

But when you break your vision down the right way and create a plan for progress, you can overcome the overwhelm.

Again, an Exceptional Sunday Assessment will help you create a plan to reach your vision.

2. Messy

Achieving your vision is usually harder – and *always* messier – than you think it will be. But if it's the right vision, it's worth it.

3. Alignment

You can't reach your vision without intentionally realigning your systems, values, and expectations toward that vision.

There's a lot in this book that can help you do that. The next two chapters will show you how to get your team members moving toward your vision.

But if you want to move further faster by realigning your ministry around a clear vision for the future, take the next step.

CLARIFY COMPELLING VISION

Clarify your vision to improve your team.

If you want help clarifying and reaching your vision for your worship ministry, schedule an Exceptional Sunday Assessment. During this call, you and a coach will talk about…

- What you would do if you and your team had the capacity, culture, and capabilities you can only dream about now…
- Where you're at right now with your time, culture, and team capabilities…
- And what might be holding you back from reaching your goals.

Even if you decide it's not the right time or best fit to work with my team, you'll get tremendous amounts of clarity and value from this call.

There's no cost to you for this session, and you can schedule it here:

https://www.worshipteamcoach.com/book-esa

Chapter 13

CREATE VISION-DRIVEN EXPECTATIONS

Be a yardstick of quality. Some people aren't used to an environment where excellence is expected.
Steve Jobs

Vision is Worthless Without This

When I first arrived at a church I served at for many years, I had a vision for…

- A professional-sounding band…
- With a front row of engaging worship leaders and vocalists who were musically confident and expressive in their worship…
- Leading powerful worship experiences for a church that was on fire for God.

CREATE VISION-DRIVEN EXPECTATIONS

Unfortunately, that vision was more of a *mirage*, because what I really had were…

- Sonic blobs of vanilla pudding…

    A band that just pounded out whatever was on the chart with no regard for the arrangement or orchestration of the instruments.

- Stand zombies…

    Lifeless musicians stared at their charts like they hadn't seen the music before that morning (because several hadn't).

- Singing statues…

    Occasionally, you might actually see one move.

And since the congregation took its cue from the stand zombies and statues on the platform…

- A church full of *screen* zombies…

    They just stared up at the screen, barely mouthing the words.

Now it wasn't always *that* painful. But we had more than our share of cringy moments.

So, was my vision unrealistic?

No, it wasn't.

We had decent musicians – even a few standout players and singers. But musically, they were *OK with being just OK*.

And spiritually, I know my team members loved Jesus (mostly), along with a lot of the congregation. But man, was it lifeless!

Here's the thing...

- My team listened to the same recordings I did to learn the songs.
- We'd watch DVDs of Paul Baloche demonstrating what good band dynamics and arranging looked like. (That's how far back this goes.)
- We even went to some conferences together and talked about how it'd be great to bring some level of that worship experience back to our church.

But week after week, it was more of the same, with only slight improvements here or there.

I didn't lack vision. But my vision was *worthless* because I didn't have a key component of visionary leadership:

Expectations.

Expectations are one of the most critical elements to make your vision a reality. But not just expectations alone. I certainly had expectations for my team:

Practice your music.
Come to rehearsal.
Grow spiritually.
Be confident and engaging.
Attend church regularly.

CREATE VISION-DRIVEN EXPECTATIONS

But what I didn't have was a critical element that would help shape my current reality into my desired future:

Clearly defined, vision-driven expectations.

For example, I wanted our music to be distraction-free and powerful as we accompanied our gathered worship every Sunday. (This is a 'vision' for a consistently better worship service).

But the expectation for preparation was more about "not sucking" and avoiding a mid-set train wreck than it was about providing dynamic worship.

We were just getting by. Again, being OK with just being OK.

I inherited this team culture, and I wasn't sure how to change it.

I was preaching to my team, *we need to practice more!* But they could've practiced for three hours a day and still sounded mediocre.

Why? Because they weren't actually learning their parts from the arrangement we were using.

Everyone just played what they wanted to.

So that had to become part of the expectations:

> *We don't just "play the chart." We learn our instrument's arranged part.*
>
> *Or, we approximate the part, but it still needs to complement and blend with the other instruments.*

So then, instead of "practice more," the expectation became clearer:

> *"Learn your part before you come to rehearsal."*

Personal practice now had a clearly defined outcome that moved us towards the vision of a fantastic-sounding band.

But even that needed to go to another level.

It wasn't enough to be a fantastic-sounding band. I wanted us to sound good because we were accompanying the 'gathered worship' of our church.

As the leader, I needed to connect the desired outcome (sound good) with a deeper aspect of the vision – to accompany our church family's 'gathered worship'.

I also did the same thing with my vocalists. My spoken expectation was, "be more expressive." But that wasn't really tied to a vision. I was just reacting to people asking why everyone on the platform looked mad or bored.

Eventually, I anchored the expectation of "be expressive" to a deeper reason. We studied and explored…

- the Biblical expressions of worship,
- the scriptural role of the lead worshiper on the platform,
- and why confidence and engagement is so critical.

Our vocalists evolved to be true lead worshipers who both worshiped God and served the congregation. Their personal preparation enabled them to know a song so well they could worship freely and engage the congregation.

Do you see how expectations that are clearly defined and tied to the vision will help you realize your desired future so much faster?

CREATE VISION-DRIVEN EXPECTATIONS

Take a look at the expectations your team is failing to meet.

- Are your expectations specific and driven by the vision?
  "Learn your instrument's specific part by rehearsal."
- Or, are they vague?
  "Practice more."

Vision-driven expectations are one of the vital leadership issues my team and I dig into with a worship leader as soon as we start work with them. Without crystal clear expectations, any visionary change they want to implement is destined to fail.

Remember what real vision is about:

Where you're going.
Why you're going there.
What it looks like when you arrive.

Vision is essentially where, why, and what.

And so expectations are a big part of the HOW. They're *how* you make progress toward your vision.

Creating Your Expectations

When it comes to communicating your vision-driven expectations (which will help you make every Sunday exceptional) we need to define three terms to help you determine how you'll articulate those clearly:

Expectations
Policies
Guidelines

We've thrown around the word *expectations* a lot in this chapter without fully defining it. So let's do that now.

An *expectation* is the belief or anticipation that a specific action or behavior will or should happen, or that a specific attitude or mindset will be maintained.

A *policy* is simply the expectation officially and explicitly defined. You also might call this a *rule*.

A *guideline* is a recommendation of conduct or procedure. It instructs rather than dictates.

Policies and *guidelines* are both a form of expectation. A *policy* specifically and prescriptively frames the expected outcome. A *guideline* describes and recommends a path to accomplish the outcome.

Here's how these terms played out on my team.

- I had an *expectation* that my team would arrive on time.
- I also had a *policy* in our handbook that stated, *"Rehearsal begins promptly at 6:30 PM. Be ready to start before that time."* This is the expectation explicitly and officially defined.
- I also gave my team a guideline: *"Plan to arrive at least fifteen minutes early to give yourself plenty of time to get set up and ready to go."*

Did they have to show up fifteen minutes early? No. If they could roll in at 6:27 PM, grab their in-ears, and be ready to go for line-check by 6:30 PM, they were adhering to the policy.

CREATE VISION-DRIVEN EXPECTATIONS

And did some people arrive *thirty* minutes early? Yes. They wanted extra time to make sure everything was working and get into the right headspace. (I loved those people the most. *You know who you are.*)

So let me summarize:

An *expectation* is the action to produce the outcome you want.

> *Show up on time.*

A *policy* clearly defines the expectation; it's prescriptive.

> *Rehearsal begins at 6:30 PM. Be ready to start before that time.*

A *guideline* suggests the path to accomplish the expectation; it's descriptive.

> *Plan to arrive at least 15 minutes early…*

So when it comes to writing your expectations, you need to decide…

- What should be framed simply as an expectation?
- What should be framed as a guideline?
- And what should be framed as a policy?

To frame an 'action producing a desired outcome' as an *expectation* means that you simply state what you expect and let the team member decide how best to meet that expectation.

To frame something as a *guideline* means giving some instruction or a course of action to help them meet the expectation.

And framing something as a *policy* means spelling out exactly how you want it done.

So let's talk about when to use which one.

Policies work well when there's a system depending on precise actions and behavior. For example, your rehearsal.

That's a system that requires team members to be present. Because of that, spelling out the exact start time is critical. And, that policy should be clear that the start time is your team's "downbeat," when the band actually begins to rehearse.

Start time should not equal *arrival time*.

Another great example of a system depending on precise actions is *team scheduling*.

A clear policy might be, *"You need to accept or decline your scheduling request at least 10 days before your scheduled service."*

That way, you're not wondering on a Tuesday if your lead guitarist will show up to rehearsal on Thursday.

If you just state the expectation – *accept or decline your scheduling request* – that's not clear enough for the system to run efficiently.

Guidelines work better for expectations that can be met in various ways or more subjectively. *Preparation* is a perfect example.

You expect team members to learn their music before rehearsal, attend and participate fully in the rehearsals, and know their parts well enough by the service so they aren't tied to the music stand or confidence monitors.

CREATE VISION-DRIVEN EXPECTATIONS

Those are your expectations.

You could create a *policy* that says, *"Everyone needs to practice 2 hours before rehearsal and another 90 minutes before services."*

But personal practice timeframes are subjective. It depends on the musician's experience, skill level, how quickly they learn the new songs, how often they've played/sang the current songs, etc.

So, in this case, a *guideline* will be more effective here.

We used the 24-hour guideline. *"After you learn the songs, play or sing through them within 24 hours of rehearsal and again within 24 hours of the service to make sure you're fresh."*

This was a guideline to help them accomplish the expectation of "be prepared and know your music." It wasn't a concrete policy. It was a suggested path to make sure their music was fresh in their minds before rehearsal and the service.

And then, finally, stating something as an *expectation* works really well in general communications.

For example, you should spell out your general expectations for potential new team members in an audition packet document or on your website.

It might read something like this:

> *We expect team members…*
> *to have a growing relationship with God.*
> *to be committed to this local church.*
> *to arrive on time for rehearsals and services.*
> *to show up to rehearsals and services with your music prepared.*
> *to treat their fellow team members and leaders with respect.*

> *to respond to scheduling requests and honor their scheduled commitments.*
>
> *to invest in their craft to get better as a vocalist, tech or instrumentalist.*[21]

Do you see how this list states the expectation, but is *not* prescriptive – that is, telling people exactly what it looks like to meet these expectations?

Nor is this list descriptive – you're not giving prospects suggestions on how to meet those expectations.

But that list of expectations is enough for a person to make an informed decision on whether she wants to take that first step and apply for the team or not.

If you required her to read a sixteen-page team handbook, with *all* your policies and guidelines, at that point in the discovery process, you might scare her away. Or, at the very least, overwhelm her.

As the applicant progresses closer to a full commitment to the worship team, that's when she'll need to know the more detailed *policies* and *guidelines* of your ministry.

Writing Vision-Driven Expectations

In our coaching program, we walk leaders through a specific, step-by-step process. It helps them determine their vision-driven expectations and then decide what should be framed as a simple expectation, a prescriptive policy, or a descriptive guideline.

---

[21] The answer is yes! You're welcome to steal this list to use in your new team member application packet. :)

CREATE VISION-DRIVEN EXPECTATIONS

I don't have space here to walk you through that process. But let me give you a 'guideline' to help you navigate this process.

You're probably one of two different types of leaders:

1. Non-detail-oriented leader.
2. Detail-oriented leader.

For non-detail-oriented leaders, they want to curl up in a ball and rock themselves to sleep at the thought of spelling out every expectation for their worship team.

Surprisingly, detailed-oriented leaders can actually get *even more* overwhelmed at this process. Because they're so detail-oriented, their minds automatically start factoring through all the different scenarios and situations that require expectations.

Detailed-oriented leaders often think they need to describe every rule for every situation in every part of their worship ministry. And yeah, that *is* overwhelming.

For both the deet-freaks and non-deet-freaks, you need to embrace the idea of "MVP"– *minimum viable product*. It's a concept used by businesses when creating a new product.

For example, a software company creating a new app won't put all the slick features and options in a version 1.0. Instead, they start by getting the absolute most important core functions right. Then, in later versions, they build out the bells and whistles.

That's a fantastic approach to create your expectations.

- Figure out your team's most important "core functions".

- Then, determine the fewest expectations needed to accomplish the core functions.
- Finally, create a "minimum viable policy" (or guideline) to communicate that desired action or behavior for each of those expectations.

In other words, keep your expectations as simple and clear as possible when starting out. You can always add to them later.

Because if your vision-driven expectations *aren't* simple and straightforward, you'll struggle with the next step: *holding your team accountable to those expectations.*

CREATE VISION-DRIVEN EXPECTATIONS

Need help with your expectations?

If you want help implementing vision-driven expectations into your ministry, schedule an Exceptional Sunday Assessment. During this call, you and a coach will talk about…

- What you want to accomplish in the next 6 - 18 months…
- Where your team and ministry is at right now…
- And what might be holding you back from reaching your goals.

Even if you decide it's not the right time or best fit to work with my team, you'll get tremendous amounts of clarity and value from this call.

There's no cost to you for this session, and you can schedule it here:

https://www.worshipteamcoach.com/book-esa

Chapter 14

UPHOLD LOVING STANDARDS

> *Camaraderie doesn't happen by accident; developing a strong sense of trust, accountability, and togetherness around team goals requires intentional effort.*
> Don Yaeger

In this section of the book, we set out to reshape your team's commitment to excellence. A few surface-level changes won't cut it. To build a team that can make every Sunday exceptional, you need to *reshape the culture*.

To do that, to truly shift the culture, you need to **clarify a compelling vision** of your desired future. Through this vision, you're beginning to define your team's culture of excellence.

But it's not enough to want a new culture.

You need to chart a path from your current reality to your vision. Show your team *how* to reach that desired future by ***creating vision-driven expectations.***

UPHOLD LOVING STANDARDS

When you do that, all your policies, rules, and guidelines will serve a purpose beyond "behavior management." Expectations show your team how to reach the vision.

Once you get crystal clear on what you expect from your team, you'll then need to ensure your team is *living out* the expectations and *living up* to the ideals of the new culture you're creating.

To do this, you'll need to **uphold loving standards.**

Uphold loving standards... that's an odd phrase, right?

It seems like it'd be more fitting to say we "uphold standards lovingly." That is, we confront and correct our team members in a loving, grace-filled manner.

How you uphold your standards is important. You want to do so with love. But it's more than that. The standards themselves are *loving*. Let's look at the different ways this proves to be true.

When you uphold the right standards, it means team members are becoming better versions of themselves – musically, relationally, and spiritually.

As you uphold your vision-driven expectations, your team members will...

- Serve the congregation better by being musically and visually confident.
- Treat you and their fellow team members with a deeper respect.
- Connect more to their wider church family as they view what they do as *service* and *ministry* instead of just *volunteering*.

- Worship and obey God more intentionally.
- Hold one another accountable to the standards. (Seriously, they will. And it's awesome!)[22]

And as you uphold your loving standards, more and more of your team will move higher up the *Levels of Engagement*. Here they are…

Leadership — Invests in others by becoming a guide
Ministry — Worships God *and* serves the congregation
Expression — Confident musicianship *and* Biblical worship
Connection — Connection with the music and other musicians
Survival — Self-absorbed because just trying to get through the song

I know, another triangle-shaped model. We'll dig deeper into these levels in the next chapter, so don't worry if this diagram isn't 100% clear.

I wanted to briefly introduce these levels now to demonstrate how raising your standards will help you improve so much more than just the musical quality of your team.

---

[22] I still remember the first time I "caught" one of my experienced volunteers gently confronting another team member about their lack of practice. It was glorious.

UPHOLD LOVING STANDARDS

As you learn about the progression from *Survival* and *Connection* upwards through *Expression, Ministry,* and *Leadership* in Chapter 15, you'll see that every step requires a *higher quotient of love.*

So, hopefully, you're convinced that holding your team to the right standards is *loving.* And now that we've all experienced that warm, fuzzy feeling of loving each other, let's talk about less warm and fuzzy stuff – the reality of accomplishing this.

When you say, "I will uphold loving standards," guess what you're really saying?

"I've gotta hold my team accountable."

The *warm fuzzies* have left the building.

Two Kinds of Accountability

Accountability. Everyone loves to talk about it. No one loves to practice it.

Let's be real. Has it ever been 'fun' to be on the giving *or* receiving end of accountability?

Nope.

And if you're a conflict-averse people-pleaser, the idea of accountability sounds even more dreadful to you.

But have hope!

If you struggle to keep your team in check and confront poor behavior, I will give you some practical steps at the end of this chapter.

But before I do, I want to talk about two primary ways you need to hold your team accountable to the expectations and standards that lead to consistent Sunday excellence.

1. Relational Accountability

This is what most leaders think of when they talk about accountability. It's the interpersonal interactions of holding each other to the team or organization's standards:

- Leader to leader
- Leader to team member
- Team member to team member
- Team member to leader

The more trust you've built among your leaders and team members, the more open and honest the conversations will be. We'll talk in-depth about this in a bit.

But let's get to the second type of accountability. And for those who naturally avoid conflict, you'll like this one.

2. Structural Accountability

This happens when you intentionally design "organizational structures" (systems, processes, etc.) to keep team members accountable.

When you…

- Build the right organizational structures that…
- Align with your vision, and…
- Reinforce your expectations…

UPHOLD LOVING STANDARDS

…those *structures* support *your standards*.

In other words, the processes and systems you create hold people in check.

And, even better news for people-pleasers…

When you have these structures, "relational accountability" gets easier. I'll talk about why that is in a moment.

But first, let's talk about what structural accountability looks like and how to build it into your worship ministry.

Vision-Aligned Systems (Take 2)

To create structural accountability, you need to align every ministry system with your vision and ensure every process supports your standards.

We already discussed vision-aligned systems in Chapter 9. But let's add a couple of examples here to demonstrate how vision alignment helps create structural accountability.

First, let's revisit the expectation that a leader wants his team to show up at rehearsal on time and prepared. Remember, the rehearsal is a process inside the major ministry system of *Preparation*.

So if a worship leader waits to start rehearsal until the last person arrives (eleven minutes late), that leader is running a process that does NOT support her standard of "arrive on time."

Let's say that same worship leader has rehearsal on Thursday evening but doesn't plan and post his setlist until Tuesday afternoon. Few team members will have enough time to practice.

His process of planning music (part of the *Set/Service Planning* system) doesn't support the standard of learning parts *before* rehearsal.

Worse yet, the setlist he posts on Tuesday contains...

- one brand new song...
- two newer ones...
- and an oldie-but-goodie (that most of the current team has never played or hasn't played in a couple years).

The leader just made it incredibly difficult for the team to adhere to his vision of "show up to rehearsal with your parts learned."

His haphazard song rotation and management process are working against that vision. The team will either...

- Throw up their hands in frustration and come in unprepared.
  Or,
- Invest an excessive amount of time to learn and relearn all those unfamiliar songs.

Neither option is good.

So, you're seeing how your systems need to align with your vision, and your processes need to support your standards, right? Those structures then help hold your team accountable to the standards.

Let's go back to the vision and expectation for on-time rehearsals.

When a person shows up four minutes late to rehearsal and the band is playing the last chorus of the warm-up song, how is he going to

UPHOLD LOVING STANDARDS

feel? That process of starting rehearsal "on-time, every time" creates social pressure on latecomers.

Now, will that eradicate tardiness?

Heck no! You lead a team of artists, creatives, and musicians. You don't get off that easy.

But it will correct the behavior of *some*. And these standards and processes make it easier to have crucial conversations[23] with your repeat offenders.

"Hey Dillon, I noticed you've come in late the last few weeks. Is everything OK?"

If you've done a good job of creating and communicating vision-driven expectations, Dillon knows he needs to be ready to play at the start time.

And the fact that he's walked in twice to rehearsals already in session has reinforced that. So he knows you're serious about this standard.

Your *structural accountability* bolsters your *relational accountability*. Because of this, you'll be starting this crucial conversation from a much stronger position.

---

[23] The term "crucial conversations" comes from a book called, *Crucial Conversations: Tools for Talking When Stakes Are High* by Joseph Grenny, Kerry Patterson, et al. They define a *crucial conversation* as "a discussion between two or more people where (1) stakes are high, (2) opinions vary, and (3) emotions run strong." So, yeah, confronting a worship team member definitely qualifies as this.

The Culture-Change Trifecta

We've defined *Upholding Loving Standards* and discussed the two kinds of accountability you'll need to implement. Next, let's examine how implementing these three outcomes – vision, expectations, and accountability – will reshape your team's culture.

To do this, let's Venn diagram it. (I love me a good Venn!)

Vision
Clarify a Compelling Vision

Expectations
Set Vision-Drive Expectations

Real, Lasting Culture Change

Accountability
Uphold Loving Standards

These three outcomes – vision, expectations, and accountability – must align for lasting culture change. Let's look at what happens when a ministry doesn't contain all three.

UPHOLD LOVING STANDARDS

Vision Only

If a leader ONLY has vision, he's daydreaming. It's the kind of leadership that a Texan would describe as "all hat; no cattle."

Daydreamer

Vision
Clarify a Compelling Vision

The vision-only leader frustrates his team members. He talks about a better future and pushes his team toward it. But there's no clear "how" to get there.

As a 'future-oriented' person, I started off in ministry high on vision and low on... *pretty much everything else*. And, *wow*, did I frustrate my team! (And the senior pastor, and the other staff, and the congregation, and...)

I learned the hard way that I needed more than just vision.

Expectations Only

Now, some leaders are fantastic at spelling out guidelines and policies. Usually, this leader is naturally detail-oriented and tends to be conscientious about rules. But since she's not highly assertive, she'll gravitate towards creating rules without thinking about vision or how to enforce them.

Non-Motivator

Expectations
Set Vision-Drive Expectations

This leader who ONLY has expectations will face some issues.

EXCEPTIONAL EVERY SUNDAY

First, there's no real motivation or pressure for her team members other than "please follow the rules." (And we know how well artists, musicians, and creatives follow the rules.)

Worse than that, this rule-oriented leader hasn't given her team any sense of purpose or meaning to the rules. There's no WHY.

Accountability Only

There are other worship leaders (albeit fewer) with more assertive personalities and leadership styles. And sometimes, this kind of leader creates an environment of high accountability without thoroughly clarifying his vision or expectations.

When a leader rolls with ONLY accountability, he imposes rules that seem arbitrary or even like moving targets. And he can come off as an authoritarian as he motivates his team.

Accountability
Uphold Loving Standards

Authoritarian

Two Out of Three Ain't... Gonna Cut It

Only having one of the three necessary outcomes won't create culture change. But neither will just two.

Take a look at what happens when the Venn gets lopsided or top-heavy.

Vision and Expectations

This is the barking, toothless Chihuahua.

UPHOLD LOVING STANDARDS

Daydreamer **Vision** Clarify a Compelling Vision — The Barking, Toothless Chihuahua — **Expectations** Set Vision-Drive Expectations *Non-Motivator*

There's nothing pushing the team to adhere to your expectations. You're relying on team members to hold themselves accountable with no extrinsic motivation. You probably have some team members who will do that. But you can probably name several right now who won't.

Vision and Accountability

This might seem like a weird combination. But it's actually not. There are plenty of assertive visionaries who don't take time to articulate the expectations they have.

This kind of leader sees her vision so clearly that she assumes others should, too. And if she's got a more dominant personality, she will hold people to that vision whether they understand it or not.

Daydreamer **Vision** Clarify a Compelling Vision

The Over-Assertive Visionary

Accountability Uphold Loving Standards

Authoritarian

If this assertive visionary leader is emotionally and spiritually unhealthy, things can get ugly.

Expectations and Accountability

A leader heavy on Expectations and Accountability, but low on Vision is the "Arbitrary Rule Maker."

When a leader doesn't take time to articulate his vision, the team won't understand the WHY behind the WHAT.

The rules may feel arbitrary, pointless, and even excessive.

Since team members don't understand the reason for a rule, they'll resent being forced to follow it.

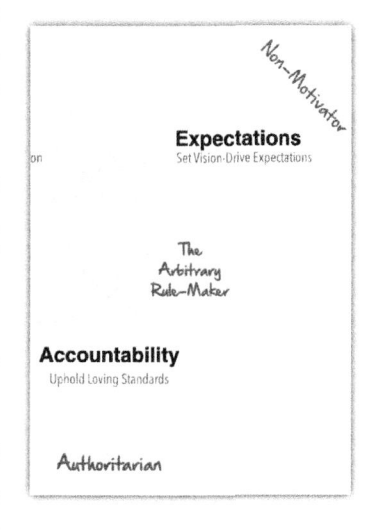

Vision gives context and purpose to an expectation. A team member still may not enjoy adhering to a particular policy, like…

"Arrive at 7:15am for sound-check…"

…but they'll understand because you've tied it to your vision…

"…so we can have a full run-through before the 9am service. That will help us lead and engage the congregation more confidently."

UPHOLD LOVING STANDARDS

In theory, it's easy to see we need all three outcomes to affect change. However, in reality, few leaders are naturally wired to include all three.

As you look at the different aspects of the Venn diagram, you're likely seeing where your natural tendencies will lead – either focusing solely on one area or favoring two while neglecting the third.

But real culture change – and actual progress towards your vision – will only happen when you have all three…

- *Vision that's clear and compelling…*
- *Expectations that drive the team towards the vision, and…*
- *Accountability that consistently and lovingly holds your team to those standards.*

Daydreamer

Vision
Clarify a Compelling Vision

The Barking, Toothless Chihuahua

Expectations
Set Vision-Drive Expectations

Non-Motivator

The Over-Assertive Visionary

The Real Culture-Changer

The Arbitrary Rule-Maker

Accountability
Uphold Loving Standards

Authoritarian

Now, if you do the work to dial in your vision, expectations, and structural accountability, you'll likely discover a very inconvenient truth:

"I still struggle to uphold loving standards!"

Of course you do. We all do. That's normal and OK! So, let's talk about why holding others accountable is so difficult.

The Avoidance of Accountability

The biggest issue with accountability is the avoidance of it – both holding others accountable and being held accountable.

Leaders and team members naturally run from it.

Patrick Lencioni writes about this at length in his brilliant book, *The Five Dysfunctions of a Team*. I would highly recommend you read it. You'll learn how the avoidance of accountability comes from and then cascades into a whole host of other dysfunctional behaviors.

Lencioni explains that the "essence of this dysfunction is the unwillingness of the team members to tolerate the interpersonal discomfort that accompanies calling a peer on his or her behavior and the more general tendency to avoid difficult conversations."[24]

Translation: *Confrontation sucks, so we don't do it.*

Calling out people on their unproductive or bad behavior is uncomfortable. But if we're going to have strong teams with high standards, we need to be willing to "enter the danger" with each other, as Lecioni calls it.

---

[24] The Five Dysfunctions of a Team, Patrick Lencioni, pages 212-213. First edition.

UPHOLD LOVING STANDARDS

He also says this in the book:

"Members of great teams improve their relationships by holding one another accountable, thus demonstrating that they respect each other and have high expectations for one another's performance."[25]

Lencioni's saying that we truly show respect for each other when we call one another out on things. This healthy confrontation and accountability is living out Philippians 2:3-4.

Be humble, thinking of others as better than yourselves. Don't look out only for your own interests, but take an interest in others, too. (NLT)

So if you don't hold your team members accountable, you're putting your comfort ahead of their growth and the team's health.

If you are building a culture where honest expectations are communicated and peer accountability is the norm, then the group will address poor performance and attitudes.

Henry Cloud

How to Confront (Without Being a Jerk or a Pansy)

I don't want to give you this daunting task of holding your team members accountable without some practical help. Remember, I said I would get you real results in this book.

---

[25] Ibid, page 215

So I'm going to give you twelve tactics to confront team members and hold them accountable. These twelve tactics are designed with a two-fold purpose.

The first purpose is to help those who are conflict-averse. I want you to have confidence when you enter tough conversations.

The second purpose is to help those who thrive on conflict conduct more grace-filled conversations.

Also, I'm going to use the context of confronting poor practice habits to make these twelve tactics even more tangible for you. But these tactics can be adapted for any situation that requires direct conversation.

12 Tactics to Confront Poor Preparation

1. Praise in public; critique in private.

This one is pretty self-explanatory. But there's a subtle trap to be aware of. If you're a leader who likes to joke with your team, 'public' criticisms can slip through veiled in sarcastic humor.

An ironic, "Wow, I can tell you really practiced that song, Tommy," might seem like a good-natured way to push Tommy to practice. But this approach is both passive-aggressive and poor leadership.

Guard your tongue against snarky comments and save critical feedback for grace-filled, one-on-one conversations.

2. Do it ASAP.

The longer you wait, the tougher it becomes. Often, you lose the window of effectiveness. Or worse, procrastination can intensify the confrontation. When we let the issues pile up, it's too easy to puke out all those grievances at once.

Remember, verbal vomit requires a lot of clean-up in Aisle U.

3. Never confront before a worship service (unless it's crucial).

If you've ever been confronted about an issue right before leading worship, you know how that can mess with your head.

I vowed never to do it to a team member unless it absolutely couldn't wait until after church.

4. Do it in person.

Or, over the phone if absolutely necessary. Never in an email or text. Written communication lacks the tone and body language that we need for grace-filled confrontation. People will read anger or other negative emotions into your words, which you didn't intend.

5. Know the person.

Different people require different approaches. For some, you'll likely need to sandwich criticism in the middle of genuine praise. But others just prefer constructive criticism straight up. Don't beat around the bush with them.

6. Be specific.

Point towards actual events and facts. Avoid vague generalizations. Instead of saying to your drummer, "You got off the click tonight," try this:

"As we were rehearsing 'Be Thou My Vision,' you got off the beat when you came in on the second verse."

7. Separate the offense from the person.

Look at these two statements:

1. "You've got a lousy sense of time."
2. "It seems like you're speeding up the tempo"

Do you hear the difference? You can just imagine how your drummer would respond to the first one. Keep it focused on *the issue* and not *the person*.

8. State how the behavior affects others.

Putting offenses in the context of how they affect the rest of the team can help the person recognize the importance of the issue.

Since we've been picking on the drummer, let's keep going. After you say…

"It seems like you're speeding up the tempo at times. I noticed it as we were running 'Be Thou My Vision.' You got off the beat when you came in on the second verse."

Then add…

"I know a little fluctuation seems OK to you. But the team is often unsure who to follow when you stray from the tempo. It makes it tough to play tight when we're not all in time together."

You could also add, *"And it can be distracting to the congregation when we're struggling to find the tempo."*

Most team members don't think about how their lack of practice affects the whole church.

UPHOLD LOVING STANDARDS

9. Use questions.

Rather than just go in with guns blazing, use questions to open the crucial conversation.

"How do you feel that song went?"

"How do you feel about _____?" is a fantastic opening for all sorts of tough conversations.

Often, the person will have already recognized their mistake or shortcoming. This gives the person the opportunity to frame the mistake from their point of view (allowing them to save face). But more importantly, it opens the door more easily to talk about the mistake from your point of view.

Good questions also keep you from jumping to conclusions about root causes or wrong solutions. Speaking of…

10. Suggest solutions.

After you ask plenty of questions and begin to understand the situation, look for potential solutions.

"Would it help to turn the click up in your monitor?"

"Are you able to take time and practice with a metronome between now and Sunday? I think that will be helpful."

But before you suggest any of your own, ask the person what he or she thinks could remedy this issue.

Just a side note. With both of the last tactics – asking questions and suggesting solutions – watch your tone. It'd be easy for these questions and suggestions to come off condescending or judgemental, even if you don't intend that.

11. Always give a reason why it's a problem.

When people know the reason behind critical feedback, they will accept it better. But if all they're told is, "You're doing it wrong," they'll eventually check out (or lash out).

Vision (the WHY) gives context to the confrontation.

12. Point to clearly communicated standards.

When you're confronting someone, tie the 'offense' back to your expectations, guidelines, policies, or values.

People are much more willing to own up to a mistake or shortcoming if they know it's an established rule or standard.

Again, when we correct behavior (accountability) without the context of crystal clear expectations, those vague 'rules' will feel unfair or arbitrary.

Without Love...

There's one more critical factor that needs to be present for accountability to work. We all know this, but it can't be left unsaid:

Your team members need to know you genuinely love them.

If a team member thinks you value the quality of music or the Sunday service over her, she won't be a part of your team for very long.

Remember, *"love...rejoices whenever the truth wins out. Love never gives up, never loses faith, is always hopeful, and endures through every circumstance."* (1 Cor 13:6-7 NLT)

In other words, love holds accountable.

UPHOLD LOVING STANDARDS

Your Next Step?

If you want help implementing the right mix of *vision, expectations,* and *accountability* into your worship ministry, schedule an Exceptional Sunday Assessment. During this call, you and a coach will talk about…

- The vision you have for your worship ministry…
- Where your ministry is at right now…
- And what might be holding you back from implementing the kind of vision, expectations and accountability that will transform your culture.

Even if you decide it's not the right time or best fit to work with my team, you'll get tremendous amounts of clarity and value from this call.

There's no cost to you for this session, and you can schedule it here:

> https://www.worshipteamcoach.com/book-esa

Part 5

CAPABILITIES
Get Your Team to Look & Sound Exceptional Every Sunday

Chapter 15

LEVELS OF ENGAGEMENT

All models are wrong, but some are useful.
George Box, British statistician

Capabilities

In this section, we focus on the *capabilities* of our team members.

To develop a team that's exceptional every Sunday, you have to focus on three critical areas.

1. Cultivating musical excellence
2. Improving your team's platform presence
3. Attracting the right people ("Five-Star Recruits")

LEVELS OF ENGAGEMENT

```
                    Essential
                    Capacity
1. Simplify Sunday Planning          1. Clarify Compelling Vision(s)
2. Build Supportive Structures       2. Set Vision-Driven Expectations
3. Triple Your Time Off              3. Uphold Loving Standards
              EXCEPTIONAL
              EVERY SUNDAY
         Engaged        Experiential
         Congregation   Worship
```

Team Doesn't Look or Sound Good Enough
Team's Consistently Exceptional EVERY Sunday

1. Cultivate Musical Excellence
2. Improve Platform Presence
3. Attract Five Star Recruits

We'll dig into each of these outcomes in detail in the following chapters.

But first, I want to focus on a team member development issue that every worship leader deals with.

The Mixed Bag

As most worship ministry leaders set out to build a team that *looks better, sounds better,* and *loves better,* they encounter an almost universal problem:

"A mixed bag of talent and maturity."

That phrase sums up the members of almost every worship ministry. There might be some outlier churches whose worship ministries are filled with exceptionally skilled people who are also emotionally healthy and spiritually mature.

My guess is *that's not your worship team.*

And that's OK. You've got a mixed bag of talent and maturity like the rest of us. As solid as my team was in certain seasons, I always had "the mixed bag." In fact, *I* was part of that mixed bag. There were times my musical skill outpaced my emotional or spiritual maturity – even as the guy hired to run the ministry.

The mixed bag is actually a good thing to embrace. It means your team has room to grow. But it also makes growing tough.

When you lead a team of...

- disparate musical and technical skills
- along with a wide-spectrum of emotional and relational levels of health
- and vastly different depths of spiritual maturity

...training and developing that team is challenging. Everyone's in a different place!

Because of this, most worship leaders take a shotgun approach to developing their team. Look back to any team development events or initiatives you attempted in the last twelve months. You probably experienced a motley mix of results at best.

As I started building what would later become our worship team member training site, Worship Workshop (https://worshipworkshop.com/), I realized any attempt to develop worship team members had to deal with this "mixed bag" reality.

As I worked with my own team and other churches, I developed a model to help worship leaders identify where their team members are and what their next stage of growth should be. It's the Levels of Engagement.

LEVELS OF ENGAGEMENT

I briefly introduced this idea to you in the last chapter.

Leadership
Invests in others by becoming a guide

Ministry
Worships God *and* serves the congregation

Expression
Confident musicianship *and* Biblical worship

Connection
Connection with the music and other musicians

Survival
Self-absorbed because just trying to get through the song

Before I tell you about each level, I want to emphasize two things.

First, **why this model is useful.** It's 'useful' because it gives language to both where your team member is at and where he/she should go next. It also helps you identify concrete ways to grow each of your team members.

The second thing I want to emphasize is **why this model is wrong.** George Box, a British statistician, said, "All models are wrong, but some are useful."

This *Levels of Engagement* model is no exception.

You'll have team members who won't fit neatly into one of these 'engagement levels.' That's OK. Models like this are tools. And no single tool can do every job, no matter how hard you try. You don't throw out a perfectly good crescent wrench just because you can't hammer a nail with it very well. (Says the mechanically inept guy who's tried it.)

Likewise, don't discount this model just because it may not fit every person on your team. Because it won't. But, it will be useful. Let me show you how.

The Worship Team Member's Levels of Engagement

These levels attempt to summarize the big steps of the journey from a self-conscious newbie to a rock-solid leader. So let's talk about each one, starting from the bottom:

The Survival Level of Engagement

The worship team member at this level is all about *surviving*.

A *Survival* level guitar player is white-knuckling it through chord changes that should be second nature. While a *Survival* level singer is scooping around trying to find a part (usually with a finger jammed in one ear).

Team members in the *Survival* phase tend to be self-absorbed. It's not because they're narcissists. They just can't get their heads out of their music stands or their eyes off their instruments to focus on much else.

Unfortunately, *Survival* players are rarely beneficial to your team. If you have some, you've likely inherited them (a previous leader let them on the team despite their limitations). Or, you've invited them in to intentionally develop them.

LEVELS OF ENGAGEMENT

And if your only drummer is at this level… *may God have mercy on your eternal soul.*

By now, your church might have reached a qualification standard that keeps out *Survival* team members. If they want to join the ministry, they'll have to improve. But, some of your higher-level team members can revert to the *Survival* phase when they're not preparing like they should.

For a team member to progress beyond this stage, he may just need to gain more skills. But ultimately, it's about investing in *personal practice*.

The amount of preparation required for this person will feel like a hefty investment for one worship set on one Sunday. But encourage him with this: the work he puts in for each Sunday is cumulative. Eventually, he'll know most of the songs. And along the way, he'll learn songs faster and have more muscle memory to bypass the long trips to the woodshed.

Also, if you're rotating fewer songs more often,[26] that early investment in personal practice will pay off even sooner.

Before long, he'll be ascending to the next level.

The Connection Level of Engagement

Connection level team members have a solid grip on their instruments. (By the way, the voice and the mixing board are included here. They're every bit an 'instrument' as is the guitar or keyboard).

---

[26] This is one of the significant ways your 'song rotation and management' system serves your team members. To dig deeper, purchase my book, The SongCycle: How to Simplify Worship Planning and Re-engage Your Church. It's available on Amazon.

These team members have moved past "just surviving" and can connect with the music and the other musicians. It's a welcome place to be – to no longer be the source of mid-service train wrecks.

Musicians who have made it here have learned to enjoy playing and singing, and they love playing and singing with the team. There's a musical camaraderie.

The problem is when the worship team member stays in the *Connection* stage. She never marries the musical enthrallment of this level to the true worship expression found in the next. For her, it's too much about the music. As a result, she won't advance to where you need her to be.

To move a team member beyond this stage, teach her that the music serves a higher purpose: to accompany the local expression of the body of Christ as they worship God together through song.

Also, personal practice at this stage is critical so she can play/sing confidently with the freedom to worship. And that will lead them to the next level...

The Expression Level of Engagement

The *Expression* level is the convergence of *confident musicianship* and *Biblical worship*. The person who reaches this level not only knows his stuff musically, but he's also able to freely engage in musical worship and show genuine expression.

This is a rewarding place to be as a worship musician. And *that* can be a problem.

Once a team member reaches this level, he often doesn't feel the need to go any higher. If a worship team member stays here, it becomes just about his musical and spiritual "fulfillment" while on the platform.

To move that player or singer beyond this personal experience phase, emphasize the dual role of the lead worshiper:

To worship God and to serve the congregation.

Serving the congregation requires modeling biblical expressions of worship. It requires dying to personal preferences of…

- closing our eyes the whole time,
- or singing spontaneous vocal riffs,
- or just getting "lost" in worship.

Those things aren't bad and can still happen on the platform. But too much of it and we lose the congregation we're trying to lead.

Which just happens to be the goal of the next level…

The Ministry Level of Engagement

Team members at the *Ministry* level are solid musicians who love God and worship Him wholeheartedly. But their worship isn't just vertical. It's *sacrificially horizontal*. They are about loving and serving the congregation whom they lead.

For instance, a worship team member at this level may study platform presence – not as a way to look good, but to better engage with and serve the church. She carries her love for the congregation off the platform, too. There's no hiding in the green room between services for her. She's out connecting with her church family.

This level also requires a conscious choice to put others on the team before herself. Things like 'showing up on time' or 'coming in prepared' aren't a *have-to*; they're a *get-to*. She knows her presence and preparation affect the rest of the team.

Imagine what your team would look like if it were full of Ministry Level worship musicians and techs. Seriously, take a second to dream about that.

It's glorious, right??

It would feel like you could stop right here. Almost. But there's one more level that every healthy worship team member should eventually rise to…

The Leadership Level of Engagement

Let's talk *Star Wars*.[27]

In the original Star Wars movie (that's *Episode IV: A New Hope*, in case you care), Luke Skywalker is the hero. Literally, he's on the hero's journey.

His two central guides through that trilogy were Obi-Wan and Yoda. But then, at the end of Episode VII, The Force Awakens, we find a wrinkly, gray, grouchy Luke.

And as the story progresses through the next movie, it's clear: Luke's no longer the hero. Instead, he (reluctantly) becomes the guide to the new hero, Rey.

---

[27] You either got really excited or just rolled your eyes. If it's the latter, please hang with me. And by the way, no one's perfect. I think you'll still get into heaven even if you're not a Star Wars fan. But chances are, your mansion of glory won't have a connected spaceport with a working Millennium Falcon like mine will. Just sayin'…

LEVELS OF ENGAGEMENT

You see where I'm going with this. At some point, every leader and team member needs to step out of the spotlight and take the mantle of a guide. This doesn't mean they no longer play or lead, but they're making room for and raising up the younger generation.

1 Chronicles 25:6 - 8 says this:

All these men were under the supervision of their father for the music of the temple of the Lord, with cymbals, lyres and harps, for the ministry at the house of God.

Asaph, Jeduthun and Heman were under the supervision of the king. Along with their relatives—all of them trained and skilled in music for the Lord—they numbered 288. Young and old alike, teacher as well as student, cast lots for their duties. (NIV)

It's pretty clear: the temple musicians were "young and old" and "teacher and student." Some were young Skywalkers; others were old Yodas.

It's painful to watch an aging tech, musician, or leader refuse to move to this level. He often becomes territorial because he's threatened by a next-generation team member.

Don't hear me wrong: his age isn't the issue! It's that he's protecting and burying his "bag of silver" that the Master gave him rather than risking and investing it for a greater return. (See Matthew 25.)

Some of the hesitation to move beyond the *Expression* and *Ministry* levels for some team members is they don't yet see themselves as leaders. But keep encouraging them toward this goal. You have team members who likely already have tremendous influence and leadership without a title or official position.

Also, remind some of your reluctant guides that 'being a leader' doesn't mean 'being in charge' of a large group of people. You need people who lean into one-to-one and one-to-few mentoring relationships. They will make a quiet but critical difference in the lives of your other team members.

A shining example of the hero becoming the guide in our 'worship world' is Paul Baloche. I've been both a participant and teacher at scores of worship events over the last twenty-five (plus) years. During that time, Paul intentionally and humbly moved into that "true elder" role:

- Encouraging younger worship leaders and songwriters.
- Championing them.
- Graciously sharing the platform with them.

That's a picture of someone who's moved into that *Leadership* level. And I imagine there was a lot more behind the scenes that I haven't seen. But his example inspired me to intentionally make the transition from "the guy" to "the guide."

From my own experience, raising up and holding space for the younger generation isn't always easy (and sometimes not fun). But, there's so much reward and fulfillment in becoming a guide.

And when leaders and team members move to this level and begin to intentionally invest in others, the Kingdom will advance and more glory will be given to the One we worship.

LEVELS OF ENGAGEMENT

You don't have to do this alone.

If you want help intentionally developing your team members up to their next level of engagement, schedule an Exceptional Sunday Assessment. During this call, you and a coach will talk about…

- The vision you have for your worship ministry…
- Where your ministry is at right now…
- And what might be holding you back from implementing the kind of vision, expectations and accountability that will transform your culture.

Even if you decide it's not the right time or best fit to work with my team, you'll get tremendous amounts of clarity and value from this call.

There's no cost to you for this session, and you can schedule it here:

https://www.worshipteamcoach.com/book-esa

Chapter 16

CULTIVATE MUSICAL EXCELLENCE

Excellence is not a skill, it's an attitude.
Ralph Marston

Excellence is to do a common thing in an uncommon way.
Booker T. Washington

Let me make sure this truth is ultra-clear:

Good musicianship *alone* won't make your team exceptional every Sunday.

But if a leader doesn't cultivate musical excellence, she'll never reach her vision of leading consistent, high-quality worship services week-after-week. That will remain just a daydream.

As we discussed in the last chapter, creating a culture of excellence goes beyond the quality of music, and really even beyond the quality of Sunday. Team members also need to grow relationally and spiritually. Because of that, you'll want to always include efforts to help them grow in non-musical areas as you develop them.

As you saw with the Levels of Engagement in the last chapter, musical growth is often the catalyst to your team becoming better worshipers, ministers, and leaders. That's why I want to focus an entire chapter on musicianship.

Cultivating musical excellence within your team requires far more than one chapter can deliver. So my goal for these next few pages is to introduce you to the three most critical elements of musicianship you need to focus on, and in which order of priority.

Also, as promised from the beginning, I'm going to give you practical tactics that you can start implementing *this week*.

Let's dive into the three most critical elements of musicianship you need to develop in your team.

1. Preparation

If you read Chapter 9, you'll probably remember *Preparation* is one of the Eight Essential Systems. "Essential" is not a strong enough adjective for this system.

Preparation is mission-critical to build a team that can make every Sunday exceptional. It's also a key component to both the musicianship of your team and their platform presence.

Also, good preparation is a "keystone habit" for your team. Charles Duhigg, in his book, *The Power of Habit,* explains that certain good habits can become the foundation and a catalyst for building other good habits. He calls these *keystone habits*.

For example, if a person develops a habit of exercising regularly, that habit can help motivate that person to eat better too.

As my team developed better practice habits, I saw other committed behaviors emerge: *showing up on time, responding to scheduling requests, attending training events,* etc. To be sure, I still had to work at cultivating commitment in those areas. But the team members' commitment to invest in better personal practice became the foundation for other highly committed behavior.

Let me say that again:

The team members' commitment to invest in better personal practice became the foundation for other highly committed behavior.

But rather than continue to tell you how crucial preparation is, let me give you three practical tactics you can start implementing – even this week – to start building that foundation of preparation.

Tactic #1: Differentiate Between Practice and Rehearsal

Can you guess what the number one preparation mistake worship teams make is?

If you guessed *"NOT* practicing," you'd be... *not* correct.

Practice-shirking slackers *are* a big problem on a lot of worship teams. But the thing I see more often in almost every size church is this mistake:

The worship team practices at rehearsal.

You might be thinking, "Isn't that the point of rehearsal... to practice?"

That's what I used to think too. But I was dead wrong.

When I arrived at my last church, I inherited a worship team that had gone without a clear leader for several months.

CULTIVATE MUSICAL EXCELLENCE

The team had deteriorated to pitifully low expectations. Like, "Just show up sometime Sunday morning with an instrument. Any instrument."

After a while, I succeeded in raising expectations for rehearsal (like, *let's actually have one*). We even got to the point where people were showing up! But it was still too often a musical dumpster fire.

So I started to look at what was really happening at the time:

Every week, my team (and I) routinely showed up to rehearsal without fully learning our music.

We neglected our *personal preparation* (practice).

So when it came time for our *relational preparation* (rehearsal), we were each still self-focused on learning.

We were *practicing* at *rehearsal*.

Then, I had an epiphany:

"What would happen if our team (including me) showed up to rehearsal with our songs actually learned?"

(I know, profound epiphany, right?)

So I set out on a crusade to get my team to prepare BEFORE rehearsal. And that was the birth of one of my most game-changing tactics:

I started to differentiate between *practice* and *rehearsal*.

I came up with a mantra to help communicate this:

Practice is personal; rehearsal is relational.[28]

I also stopped calling our mid-week preparation event *practice* and referred to it instead as *rehearsal.* (Language shapes culture.)

To help you and your team implement this concept, I have a 'cheat sheet' that gives six differences between practice and rehearsal. Use this to start some meaningful dialog with your team about their practice habits.

Download The Practice vs. Rehearsal Cheatsheet by going to www.worshipteamcoach.com/pvr

This concept of 'NOT practicing at rehearsals' is so foundational that it's one of the first things my coaches and I work on with leaders when they join our coaching program.

Usually, we find worship leaders' teams are in one of three places with preparation:

- **They have an unhealthy culture of not practicing** due to busyness, lack of commitment, or even musical ignorance.
- **They have a team that practices OK.** But the leader knows if she raised the bar, she could spend more time at rehearsals gelling musically and working on platform presence and engagement.
- **They have a musically solid team who learns their songs.** *But,* the leader wants to get to that *next level of exceptional.* For some, that might be playing with a click

---

[28] Remember back in Chapter 12 when we discussed creating short, memorable statements (mantras, mottos, etc.) to communicate a critical part of the vision succinctly? This is one of those.

or memorizing music. For others, it's just about playing tighter and being more purposeful with parts.

Some leaders come into the coaching program and say, "Nah, Jon, my team practices alright." But when we dig in and analyze their team's behavior and Sunday results, even "solid" teams need to grow in the area of preparation.

Tactic #2: Run Practice-Required Rehearsals

If you're going to differentiate between practice and rehearsals, you have to run your rehearsals in a way that pushes your team to practice before they show up.

So let me give you five quick-win tips to run a "practice-required" rehearsal.

1. Stop listening to songs at rehearsal.

If you listen to songs (or stop to give individual team members time to listen to their parts) during rehearsal, you're enabling "practice at rehearsal."

It was a line in the sand when I told my team we would no longer listen to songs at rehearsal. I got plenty of pushback. And yes, we had rough rehearsals where I was sorely tempted to stop and listen to the recording.

But that forced us to do a better job of listening and learning the songs on our own time. And I kept repeating the mantra, *Practice is personal; rehearsal is relational.*[29] Eventually, most of my team got on board. Or jumped ship.

2. Be the most prepared person in the room.

You need to model good preparation. If you show up 80% prepared, your team will show up 60% prepared.

But besides leading and modeling, there's another huge reason for investing time into learning your parts really well:

If you don't know your stuff, you can't focus on their stuff.

When you don't practice enough, you're too focused on your own parts to catch their mistakes or suggest improvements.

3. Leave time for a R.E.A.L.™ run-through.

R.E.A.L.™ stands for *Run Elements As-if Live*. So after you rehearse the songs, save time at the end for a full run-through of the songs. But, add to this run-through as many "real" conditions as possible:

- Turn on the confidence monitors.
- Push the stands low and to the side (or remove them completely).
- Face the congregation seats and imagine it's a full house.
- Run your segues.

---

[29] When it comes to repeating vision or culture reinforcing statements like this, you need to repeat them constantly. When you're ready to punch yourself in the face because you're sick of hearing it, keep finding opportunities to repeat it. Then, when your team starts mimicking you and making fun of the statement, you now know that *they know it*. Congratulations, you've just won! Let them mock you.

CULTIVATE MUSICAL EXCELLENCE

- Work on platform presence.

You'll need to manage your rehearsals well if you're going to accomplish this run-through. But on Sunday, you'll be so glad you did.

4. 80/20 your rehearsal.

We don't have space to discuss the Pareto principle (aka 80/20 principle). Just ask Google. But let me explain how you can apply it to your rehearsals.

Chances are, 20% of your songs will require 80% of your rehearsal time: a new song, a complicated section, a new arrangement, etc.

Because of that, don't spend time focusing on the 80% of the already solid music. Instead, invest the bulk of your rehearsal time in the 20% of the song sections that need the most work.

As you implement the SongCycle[30] – which means you're rotating fewer songs more often – this will be even easier. In fact, your team will know some of your songs so well that you can just skip them altogether. Or, you can just run the "tops and tails" (that is, the intro and the outro, then go into whatever segue you have planned).

5. Start on time. End on time. *Every time.*

Nothing enables uncommitted behavior like waiting to start rehearsal until everyone arrives. Implement a policy that your posted start time is also your 'downbeat' – when you start your warm-up song. And when the clock strikes that downbeat time, start regardless of who's not there.

Remember our conversation about culture?

---

[30] See Chapter 8.

You get what you tolerate.

If you tolerate latecomers, you'll have a team full of tardy turkeys who waste *your* time and the *other team member's* time – those who are dedicated enough to arrive early.

Also, *ending on time* is equally important. If you don't, your team will grow to resent rehearsals (and you). But more importantly, the tighter time frame keeps you and the team from backsliding into the old habit of practicing songs at rehearsal.

Tactic #3: Plan to Prioritize Preparation

Finally, the third tactic you can start implementing this week is to plan schedules and music sets in a way that prioritizes preparation. What I mean by that is this:

Your Sunday planning can actually work against good preparation.

Here are four common planning mistakes that keep your team from being as prepared as possible.

Mistake #1: Too many songs to learn or relearn.

We've already touched on this concept of rotating fewer songs more often and limiting the number of new songs you introduce.

If you don't curb your song rotation, your team will always be required to learn and relearn multiple songs every Sunday. That takes up precious time that few of your volunteers have to give.

Mistake #2: Songs and setlists aren't available soon enough.

You can't expect to give your team a setlist on Tuesday and be ready for rehearsal on Thursday. So if you're posting your setlist the same week it's scheduled, I want to push you to start planning your songs

CULTIVATE MUSICAL EXCELLENCE

at least two weeks in advance. And eventually, even further out than that.

We teach a four-week "batch process" technique to our coaching clients.[31] With this process, you can still work around sticky issues like closing songs and other elements that need to be tied to the message theme.

By planning and posting your songs sooner, you'll start to eliminate the "I don't have time" excuse team members give for not practicing.

Mistake #3: No default song forms.

"Why bother practicing. You change the song every time we do it!!"

More than one team member leveled that accusation at me during my early years. *Guilty as charged.*

To serve my team better and make it easier for them to practice...

- I created default song forms (or sequences) for every song.
- Also, I had a designated key (or keys, if different leaders needed different keys) for every song.
- And I usually stuck with the same arrangement (that included a reference recording) for as long as we did the song.

This accomplished a few things:

- It reduced excuses for not practicing.
- It also helped my team remember songs in our active rotation (SongCycle).

---

[31] We discuss batch processing in more detail in Chapter 8: Simplify Your Sunday Planning.

- It made it easier to make changes when we did want to adjust the arrangement.[32]

Mistake #4: Clarify charts & parts.

You will enable poor practice if you don't define what each team member is supposed to learn.

You need to provide…

- Reference recordings (in the right key) or rehearsal mixes so team members can listen to the songs.
- Rehearsal notes (or band notes) to spell out what they need to know before rehearsal.
- Charts that match the arrangement.

Also, consider different learning styles and musical knowledge when it comes to charts. I provided chord charts, lead sheets, and lyric sheets for my team. And don't forget your auditory learners. For some musicians, the recording *is* their chart.

Believe it or not, we're just scratching the surface about how you can leverage preparation to grow a team that's consistently excellent every Sunday.

I wish space allowed me to give you more, but it doesn't. If you want to explore what it would be like to overhaul your team's practice habits, schedule an Exceptional Sunday Assessment at https://www.worshipteamcoach.com/book-esa.

---

[32] It's easier to make changes to an existing song structure than try to define a new one every time.

CULTIVATE MUSICAL EXCELLENCE

Now, the bulk of this chapter has been spent on *Preparation* because it's so critical to cultivating musical excellence.

But I wouldn't be delivering on my promise to help you get results if I didn't invest some space for the next two critical elements of building a musically excellent team.

2. Team Musicianship

Team musicianship is about how individual singers and instrumentalists play and sing together. It involves…

- Learning purposeful parts
- Intentional arranging and orchestration[33]
- Listening to each other
- Playing in time together

… and more. Rather than go in-depth with team musicianship, I thought I'd give you a handy checklist you can use to assess how well your team is doing in this area.

---

[33] Don't let those $10 musical terms intimidate you. We have programs to help your team learn how to 'self-arrange' and play purposeful parts. You'll also learn how to 'arrangement hack' popular worship songs in order to sound like the recording without needing to duplicate it perfectly. This will save you and your team time (and money – since you won't need to buy all the tracks).

The Worship Team Musicianship Checklist

Use this checklist as a tool to find ways to level-up the musicianship of your worship team members. But be careful not to use this as the "definitive guide" for where your team needs to grow as musicians. Every worship team is different. This checklist is a starting point for you and your team to explore how to go deeper as musicians.[34]

- ❏ Your team members can successfully play/sing with a click or a metronome without getting off tempo.
- ❏ Your team understands how to play/sing on tight and together.
- ❏ Each team member understands all the different roles his/her instrument might play in any given arrangement.
- ❏ Your team members understand how to self-arrange – that is, fit into the rhythmic and sonic spectrums of a song without stepping on other players' parts or roles.
- ❏ Your team members understand "laying out" (not playing or singing) as a valuable musical contribution to certain portions of a song or even portions of a set.
- ❏ Each instrument understands how to listen to and complement others in the band – both rhythmically and sonically.
- ❏ Each team member listens to the scheduled music as part of their preparation.

---

[34] Go here to download a PDF of this: www.worshipteamcoach.com/team-musician-checklist

CULTIVATE MUSICAL EXCELLENCE

- ❑ Your team prepares prior to rehearsal, learning their parts to a level that allows them to fully participate in rehearsal without being hindered.
- ❑ You provide a reference recording of what you want the song to sound like, so each team member understands the part he/she needs to learn.
- ❑ Your team fully participates in rehearsals, sound-checks, warm-ups and services – coming in prepared and on-time so you can begin your rehearsals at your posted start time.
- ❑ You plan songs far enough in advance so team members can practice prior to rehearsal.
- ❑ You provide charts and recordings for each song at least one week before the service so your team has time to prepare.
- ❑ You write preparation/rehearsal notes for each song to enable your team members to practice more effectively.
- ❑ You have a document (policy/guide/handbook) explaining what your musical expectations are for each instrument.
- ❑ You offer regularly scheduled training events throughout the year to develop the skill and musicianship of your team members.
- ❑ You have a document (policy/guide/handbook) explaining what your expectations for preparation are–this includes personal practice, and rehearsal and soundcheck participation.
- ❑ You plan out the flow and focus of rehearsals ahead of time.
- ❑ Your team understands how critical solid musicianship is for accompanying the "sung worship" of your church.

3. Individual Skill

While you're getting your team to practice more effectively and foster good team musicianship, you'll also want to focus on this third element of cultivating musical excellence.

I put this in last place intentionally. Too often, this is where worship leaders *start* when trying to cultivate musical excellence.

It makes sense. If your players and singers get better, Sunday will sound better, right?

Unfortunately, no.

I had incredibly gifted and skilled musicians on my team at different times.

- One of my keyboardists was the musical director for a theater company.
- One of my singers made it to the blind auditions of The Voice.
- I even tried to convince one of my young drummers to move to Nashville to be a session player. He was *that* good.

They were brilliantly talented musicians.

CULTIVATE MUSICAL EXCELLENCE

But there were times – even with such talent – when we sounded cluttered and chaotic. There were two reasons:

1. Good musicians often think they don't need to practice.

Instead, they "wing it." The improvised parts they played or sang may have been correct (and even impressive).

But too often, those parts didn't complement the other singers and instruments. Or worse, they trample all over the rest of the band. And this sometimes happens because…

2. Talented *solo* musicians don't always make good *ensemble* musicians.

I had a keyboard player for a hot minute who could play every Elton John and Billy Joel song ever charted. He could also whip out jazz standards like a pro.

But then, on the first Sunday he played with us, it was an unmitigated disaster. However, I'm going to wait to tell you that story in Chapter 18. It's a doozie.

Because of experiences like this, I would take a team of average musicians who know how to…

- listen to each other…
- stay on time…
- and play purposeful parts…

…over a team of self-focused musically-talented superstars. Always!

Now, with all that said, it's still important to develop the individual skills of your instrumentalists and singers. But it has to be in conjunction with *good preparation* and *solid team musicianship*.

One of the resources we've developed to help you grow your preparation, team musicianship, and individual skills is *Worship Workshop*. (http://worshipworkshop.com/)

When you join our coaching program, you'll also get access to *Worship Workshop* for your entire team. And we'll work with you to create a customized implementation plan to make the most of *Worship Workshop's* many courses and classes.

I trust this chapter has given you a hefty amount of practical tactics and tools you can use to cultivate musical excellence. If you'd like our help to implement these concepts, schedule a time to talk with one of our coaches.

CULTIVATE MUSICAL EXCELLENCE

Get a better sounding band.

If you want to explore how we can help you elevate your worship team's musical excellence, schedule an Exceptional Sunday Assessment. During this call, you and a coach will talk about…

- What you want your team's capacity and culture to look like in the next six to eighteen months…
- Where they're at right now with practice, team musicianship, and individual skill…
- And what might be holding you back from reaching your goals.

Even if you decide it's not the right time or best fit to work with my team, you'll get tremendous amounts of clarity and value from this call.

There's no cost to you for this session, and you can schedule it here:

https://www.worshipteamcoach.com/book-esa

Chapter 17

DEVELOP PLATFORM PRESENCE

You don't have to change who you are, you have to become more of who you are.
Sally Hogshead

Your platform worship will never exceed your private worship.
Jon Nicol

Stop me if you've heard this one...

What has 14 arms, 7 noses, and never moves?

.
.
.

Your worship team!

Ba-da-CHING!

OK, that was a terrible joke. But unfortunately, it might be partially true.

DEVELOP PLATFORM PRESENCE

And it might be even worse... the noses are all buried in music stands, and those arms just aren't sure what to do.

Now, you likely have some team members who are engaging and expressive on the platform.

But chances are, you have too many team members who are more *statue* than *lead worshiper*.

Remember earlier in the book when I talked about getting your team to look better, sound better, and love better?

Worship Team Vocalists...

...a little too focused on the confidence monitor.

This is about *looking better*.

Some people are naturally inclined toward expressiveness, while others are more stoic.

But your team can develop an engaging platform presence, even if some are more subdued than other team members.

And those comfortable with physical expression on the platform still need to intentionally grow and mature in this area.

First, let's talk about why physical expression matters. Then, we'll talk about what 'platform presence' is and how to develop it.

Why Expression Matters

There's a myth among too many worship team members that goes something like this:

"We need to disappear on the platform."

This myth comes from a well-intentioned place. We're worried our movement and expression will draw attention to ourselves.

We all know worship leadership isn't just musical. It's also *visual.* Excellent worship leadership requires visual leadership.

And visual leadership requires *expression.*

Think about it. Have you ever seen a pastor deliver a message with little physical expression? It's painful. Likewise, a worship team member's lack of expression is actually distracting. Here's why:

Our platform presence and expression should *reinforce* what and why we're singing.

Even though the congregation may not be able to articulate it, they'll pick up on the incongruence between what an unengaged team member is singing and her lack of expression.

For example, if someone is singing about the joy of the Lord, but their face looks like someone spit in their Cheerios, that's incongruence.

DEVELOP PLATFORM PRESENCE

And that incongruent expression is actually more distracting than genuine expressiveness.

Also, *nobody* wants to follow somebody they don't believe!

Another reason expression matters is this: *We're hosts of an important celebration.*

Our guest of honor is Jesus. We aren't there to try to steal his glory. But that doesn't mean we disengage and try to be invisible.

Imagine being invited to a birthday party for a friend you know, but at another person's house you've never met.

You knock on the door.

The host answers and says a quiet hello, but he's looking at your shoes.

He then invites you in with a terse twitch of his head and walks away, leaving you to close the door behind you. You're then left to make your own introductions and find your way to the guest of honor.

How welcomed do you feel?

Leading gathered worship requires us to engage our guests, so we can enthusiastically point them to Jesus.

We have a twofold purpose as lead worshipers: *We worship God, and we help others worship God.*

The role is actually priestly.

Just like the Levites would set up the tabernacle in the Old Testament, we help create an environment that encourages people to worship

God with their whole being. Part of creating that environment is to encourage worship through our visual leadership.

That's why worship leaders need to invest in their worship team's platform presence.

What Is Platform Presence?

Platform presence is two sides of the same coin:

One side is Biblical expressions of worship. The other is intentional and engaging platform action.

The first side contains all the different expressions demonstrated throughout scripture: bowing, standing, shouting, raising arms, clapping, and so on.

These are *external expressions* of *internal convictions*.

The other side of the platform presence coin is knowing how to lead from a stage. It involves both intentional action to engage the congregation visually and also physical movement to match the music and mood.

A quick side note.

I purposefully use the term 'platform presence' instead of 'stage presence.'

First, I chose to call our stage a 'platform.' That differentiated between it being a place to minister and serve versus a place to perform.

Second, there's a significant overlap with 'stage presence' taught in the performance arts. But the lead worshiper role isn't just about

DEVELOP PLATFORM PRESENCE

engaging a congregation (or *audience,* in stage presence vernacular). It's also about genuinely worshiping God.

If you want to use the terms 'stage' and 'stage presence' with your team, that's great. I'm not the holy nomenclature police. It was simply a choice I made to be more intentional with language, because of how much language shapes culture.

So let's talk about what goes into creating intentional platform presence.

The Elements of Platform Presence

Here are the elements for exceptional platform presence expressed in an equation:

Preparation + Confidence + Experience x A Worshiping Heart = Platform Presence.

Or, if you want to get mathy: $WH(P+C+E) = PP$

Let me touch on each of these elements briefly:

Preparation

We can't physically engage when we're mentally preoccupied. *Freedom of the heart starts with freedom from the chart.*

If you want expressive lead worshipers (vocalists and instrumentalists), your team has to put in the practice to know their music.

You also need to invest time into studying and teaching the different biblical expressions, so your team fully understands why they're doing what they're doing on the platform.

We don't have space to go into what those expressions are. But in our team member training program, *Worship Workshop*, we teach the different Biblical expressions of worship in two short courses called *Lead Worshiper 101* and *Lead Worshiper 201*.

Confidence

Once your team internalizes the songs, that will give them a mammoth dose of confidence. But there's a confidence that transcends musical preparation.

If someone is called to the worship team, they're called to be confident on the platform.

You've been delegated authority by your church's governing body to lead the congregation in worship. In turn, you've delegated authority to your team to be lead worshipers.

They have to understand their role isn't just singing or playing, it's also *visual leadership*. Help them embrace their calling and learn to step into it with a sense of healthy authority and confidence.

Experience

Even the most outwardly expressive people still need intentional platform practice over time.

Just like with athletics, it's all about "the reps."

Your team needs to clock some real hours practicing biblical expressions of worship and physical platform movements. That's the only way for some of these movements to feel natural.

Encourage your team to view platform presence as something they can improve upon and grow more natural doing it.

DEVELOP PLATFORM PRESENCE

Bonus Tip: You can double your team's 'reps' if you practice your physical expressions and visual leadership movements during rehearsals and soundchecks.

(It's legal in your state. I checked.)

Now, if you just had these three elements – *preparation, confidence, and experience* – you could look great and offer visual leadership. But that's not enough.

A Worshiping Heart

We need a worshiping heart. A worshiping heart is a multiplier for each of those other elements.

It's the "love factor" from 1 Corinthians 13: *without love (or a worshiping heart), we're just noisy gongs and clanging cymbals.*

And a worshiping heart doesn't just love God.

Love for God should always result in love for the congregation you're leading.

(Better read that last sentence again. And start repeating it to your team often. I wish I had promoted this idea more when I was leading full-time.)

Think about it. If your team truly loves the congregation they're serving, they'll be better lead worshipers.

A worshiping heart is critical. And because of that, your team's platform worship will never exceed their private worship.

They might...

- prepare...

- grow in confidence...
- and gain the experience to lead expressively...

...but without love – both for God and for their local church – it's just a show and a chance to get 'the feels.'

Where Do I Start??

Let me give you some practical steps to level-up your team's platform presence – even as early as this week.

Here are three action steps to give your team:

1. Internalize the music.
Memorized is best. But a significant step towards memorization is practicing each song enough so just an occasional glance at the chart is all that's required. That way, the music stand can go low and off to the side.

2. Study your songs.
Look at the lyrical content. What are the appropriate physical expressions that match the truth of the song and your response to it?

And notice the flow. What movements might match the music and mood in each moment?

3. Worship in private.
Once you know your songs, use those to have a personal worship time.

But before you have those songs ready, worship with other songs that you can play or sing from the heart – the ones you know intimately.

DEVELOP PLATFORM PRESENCE

As you worship with those songs, physically move and express. Remind your team that this might not seem natural at first, but God doesn't mind that we practice our worship.

And keep reminding them that their *platform worship will never exceed their private worship.*

Get a better looking team.

OK, we can't give you a stage full of fashion models. But if you want to explore how we can help you elevate your worship team's platform presence, schedule an Exceptional Sunday Assessment. During this call, you and a coach will talk about…

- What you want your team's platform presence to look like in the next six to eighteen months…
- Where they're at right now with expression, confidence, and visual leadership…
- And what might be holding you back from reaching your goals.

Even if you decide it's not the right time or best fit to work with my team, you'll get tremendous amounts of clarity and value from this call.

There's no cost to you for this session, and you can schedule it here:

https://www.worshipteamcoach.com/book-esa

Chapter 18

DEEPEN YOUR BENCH

Growth is the only evidence of life.
John Henry Newman

If you're going to build a team that can make every Sunday exceptional, you need to grow your team with…

- ***The right number of people,*** so you can create a sustainable rotation in every position.
- ***The right people with skills*** who meet or exceed your *Exceptional Every Sunday* standards. (See Chapter 13.)
- ***The right people with the quality of character*** who will fit the healthy team culture you're working to build. (See Chapter 11.)

Even with that said, I need to warn you: growing your worship team *numerically* is a risky business.

While you may want (or desperately *need*) more team members, you know that new people will change your team. Even if the change is for the better, you may have other team members who feel threatened or even get territorial.

DEEPEN YOUR BENCH

And that's why building a new team member growth system that aligns with your vision is critical.

In this chapter, you'll learn…

- Why should grow (your *Philosophy of Growth*)
- What's at risk if you grow with the wrong people
- Who the right people are (your *Five-Star Recruits*)
- What the most critical elements of a qualification process are (your *7 Qs*)

Let's start with *why* you should grow.

Your Philosophy of Growth

Before you start trying to attract, qualify, and invite new team members, it's important to develop and clarify your philosophy of growth.

That's just a fancy way to say, "Here's why we're growing."

To you, it's obvious. *But…*

You will have people on your team who essentially don't want to grow. They want to stay "us four and no more." So, you need a thoughtful response ready for those team members. But this goes far beyond just being ready to address complaints.

Determining your philosophy of growth is important to help align this system with your vision. Also, as we progress through this chapter, you'll learn that numerically growing your team is about more than just filling gaps on your roster.

7 Reasons to Grow

So let me give you seven reasons why a worship team needs to grow. And I'll also share with you a really lousy reason to grow that too many churches use.

Some of these seven reasons may not fit the vision of your church or ministry. But I trust most of them will help you develop your philosophy of growth. Here they are in no particular order. (Other than the lousy reason. I saved that stinker for last.)

Reason #1: Create Mentoring Relationships

As you add musicians, you can create potential mentoring and discipling relationships. If you have older or more experienced people on your team, you can afford to bring in younger and less experienced instrumentalists, techs, and singers to develop them.

"Generational transference" is the passing down of wisdom and knowledge from one generation to another. It's ancient wisdom seen several places in scripture.

But in 1 Chronicles 25:6-8 – which we looked at earlier – we see generational transference specifically for worship and music.

This passage talks about those appointed to serve as musicians in the temple. There's clearly a system of training and development: "Young and old alike, teacher as well as student...."

Reason #2: Raise the Bar

As you increase the number of instrumentalists, techs, and singers, your overall skill level increases. You'll be able to do more musically as you grow.

And, as the team's overall capacity grows, your higher standards will attract better-quality team members. I saw this happen in my ministry. As our Sunday quality increased, it attracted higher caliber musicians. Good musicians want to be a part of good teams.

Reason #3: Develop Specialists

When you add more team members, it allows people to be *specialists* versus *generalists*. Your team members get to serve from their strengths rather than stay stuck filling a spot where they're not as gifted. I see this all the time in worship teams:

- An acoustic guitarist who's dabbled with the bass gets stuck playing it because no one else can.
- A worship leader is forced to play acoustic guitar or piano, when she might be a far better leader if she could just lead vocally.
- A gifted sound tech also happens to play drums, but not that well. But because of gaps on the team, she agrees to play drums. But that leaves the mix to a mediocre tech who'd probably be better at running lights.

Don't get me wrong, I love a good "utility player." But even your utility players have their sweet spot. Growing your team helps move everyone deeper into their wheelhouse.

Reason #4: Serve at a Healthier Pace

This is a big one. We've talked a lot about your capacity as a leader and taking enough time off. Your team members need time off, too.

Even if they don't want it!

You probably have people on your team who say they "love" to sing or play and want to be scheduled every week. But fast forward eighteen months, and the same player will dread rehearsal and no longer like attending church.

Why? He's burned out!

More team members mean people can serve at a sustainable pace. (Including you.)

But the pace isn't just about sustainability. It's 'healthier' because it guards against *entitlement*. When someone regularly shares a team role with one, two, or three other people – and *not* serving every week – they're far less likely to feel entitled or be territorial about their position.

Reason #5: Diversify Your Musical Styles

Bringing in more musicians allows you to broaden the musical styles of your team.

If you're playing the same four chords with the same five instrumentalists week after week, month after month, it all sounds homogenized.

Don't be afraid to explore new music styles as your team grows.

Reason #6: Multiply and Send Out

Growing your team enables you to send out people to additional campuses, church plants, or even to a different church God might be calling someone to.

DEEPEN YOUR BENCH

We need to have the mindset that we are preparing people to go out and do Kingdom work. You're not there to build a worship team empire.

Reason #7: More People Can Serve

"We have too many people serving in this church." Said no pastor, ever.

Now, this one can be dangerous if your church has the *"ANYONE* can serve on the worship team!" mindset. But most teams need more people to…

- Create a sustainable rotation of team members that gives optimal time off to everyone.
- Lead different aspects of the worship ministry.
- Fill support roles and do other administrative work.
- Help develop current team members and train potential ones.

Also, if you've led a worship ministry for more than a few years, you know the seasons of abundance and scarcity. Adding team members helps you be prepared for unexpected departures from your team. Because here's a fact:

Everyone will leave your team *eventually*.

As you think about these reasons to grow and add team members, you may think of other reasons that you'll want to add to your philosophy of growth.

But let me give you a lousy reason that too many churches believe.

A Really Bad Reason to Grow

Throughout my time as a worship pastor, I've had a number of team members who believed the worship ministry existed so they had a "platform to share their gifts."

(Sorry, I just threw up in my mouth a little.)

The worship ministry isn't a talent show. And when churches have this mindset, it feeds people's egos and creates a sense of entitlement. The worship ministry is a place for people to use their gifts and talents to serve the church and worship God.

Creating Your Philosophy of Growth

If you've never clarified why you want to grow, use this section as a catalyst to start making a list.

(Heck, you can even just copy the reasons here and call it your first draft. I won't tell anyone.)

Now, something to keep in mind. This philosophy of growth helps defend your desire to add team members. But implicit in your philosophy are reasons to *limit* who joins the team, too. And in a moment, I'm going to help you define more directly who the "right fit" people are and who they are not.

But before I do, I want to share with you a massive mistake I made by inviting a 'wrong fit' person to join my team.

Don't Jeff-Up Your Team

"Jeff wants to play on our worship team!"

Jeff[35] was a pro-level keyboard player who had recently left another church and had started attending mine. My current team members who knew him passed along this juicy piece of intel.

As much as I wanted a player of his caliber, something wasn't sitting right. But I proceeded to "audition" Jeff and invite him on the team.

That series of events would lead to a colossal disaster that I'll tell you about in a minute. But first, here's WHY it was a disaster.

I made multiple blunders when bringing Jeff on the team:

- I didn't require a minimum commitment to our church.
- I didn't run him through our full audition process.
- I chose to ignore red flags.
- I let myself be swayed too much by talent.
- I started him too quickly on the team.

Let me explain each of these blunders...

I Ignored Our Minimum Commitment Guideline

Because Jeff was so good, I was afraid he would get antsy and find another church to play in. So I ignored my "be a part of the church for six months" guideline.

After the nightmare that ensued with Jeff, the *guideline* became a *policy*.

---

[35] Not his real name. And, my deepest apologies to all the great and wonderful "Jeffs" out there.

I Didn't Run the Full Process

Because he was so good, I only put him through one step of our audition process, a loosely-run interview where I listened to him play.

> *By himself.*
> *Without a band.*
> *Without a click.*
> *And with songs he picked out himself.*

Soon enough, I would find out how big a blunder this actually was.

And, the fact that he was a little irritated that he even had to "audition" at all should've been a clue to me about what lay ahead.

Which was my next shortcoming...

I Ignored Warning Signs

Because Jeff was so good, I chose to ignore critical warning signs telling me he was NOT a good fit for our team.

That's the power of a good audition process. It creates enough time, requires multiple steps, and invites different people's perspectives – all of which help you to identify and address the red flags.

But I ignored them for one, big (dumb) reason...

Jeff was so dang talented on the keys!

I Assumed the Talent Would Overcome the Toxic

One day after church, before I had invited Jeff on the team, he came up and started playing on our stage piano. He was whipping out jazz standards, Elton John, Billy Joel, and every 80s piano ballad that ever hit the charts.

DEEPEN YOUR BENCH

My team was enamored by him. "You've GOT to get him to join us, Jon!"

Jeff was eating up this attention from everyone gathered around him.

I started seeing it then and saw it more as we interacted in the coming weeks: Jeff had some character issues.

But, I ignored them in favor of talent, which taught me a difficult lesson: ***Toxic trumps talent. Every time.***

That is, a toxic personality or significant character issue can never be counterbalanced by the talent that person brings to the team. The character issue will *always* end up costing the worship ministry more than it gains from the person's skills and abilities.

I Prematurely Platformed Him

After Jeff's quasi-audition, I scheduled him almost immediately. Unfortunately, Jeff came from a church that didn't have in-ears, didn't use clicks, and learned the music during rehearsal.

We had in-ears, used a click, and we learned our parts at home.

And yes, all this led to disaster.

A Jeff-ing Train Wreck

The first rehearsal with Jeff was a nightmare. Everything took twice as long.

- We started late because Jeff didn't know how to use in-ears.
- Once we got started, he made such a fuss about the in-ears I finally gave in and hooked up a powered monitor speaker to his personal mixer.

- We stopped and started every song that had a piano intro because Jeff couldn't sync with the click.
- We frequently had to ask him to stop playing or play less in certain parts. He was drowning out the entire band.

By the end of rehearsal, he admitted that he should probably listen to the songs and work on his parts before Sunday. We all left that marathon rehearsal emotionally exhausted.

Unfortunately on Sunday, both the warm-up and service were a sitcom rerun of the rehearsal.

- He didn't play any of the actual parts he was supposed to.
- He got off the click track.
- He stepped all over the bass player.
- And both guitarists.
- And his rhythms clashed with the drummer.

On one song, his part was so completely off the beat that my co-worship leader had to stop the song and start over.

During the actual service!!

Thankfully, Jeff's tenure on our team wasn't long. By what I can only say was God's great mercy, Jeff took a new job and moved away shortly after joining our team.

My failure to qualify Jeff wasn't just a disservice to my team and church, but it was also a disservice to Jeff. He knew the train wreck was his fault.

And while his musical hubris might be blamed, I had to take full responsibility for not qualifying and preparing him to fit in with our team.

Trust the Process

When Jeff joined the team, I had a multi-step process in place to qualify new team members. But I didn't follow it.

And after that debacle, I decided to trust the process with *everyone*, no exceptions.

I was ultimately thankful for that situation with Jeff. It forced me to look at our new team member onramp closely and add some much-needed steps to the audition and orientation processes.

So here's the question: Can you trust *your* process?

Is it built out in a way to invite the right people in and repel the wrong people? That is, is each step of your audition system designed to determine if someone is the right fit or not?

Before you can fully answer that, you need to be crystal clear on who your 'right fit' people are and aren't. And that's where our "five-star" system comes in.

The Right Fit: *Who Are Your Five-Star Recruits?*

When bringing in new team members, you want to ensure you get it right. Why? Because it's easier to disqualify someone before they join the team than remove them after.

Did you catch that? Let me say that again:

It's easier to disqualify someone before they join the team than remove them after.

If you've had a person in your worship ministry that your predecessor should have never allowed on the team, then you know what I'm talking about. Or, if *you've* ever invited someone in who didn't fit your team, you know how potentially damaging it is to your team.

To help determine if an applicant will be a good fit, let me walk you through our version of the "Five Cs." Think of these qualities as star ratings. They'll help you find and attract your Five-Star Recruits.

These descriptors will probably sound familiar to you. Lots of churches and organizations use variations of this list of "Cs". I've modified them after building my own new team member qualification process and helping other leaders build theirs.

Before we look at each of these five stars, let me clarify a few things:

First, these qualities can be put in any order you want, because they ALL matter.

For example...

- A potential recruit may have high personal integrity (Character), but she's more of a lone ranger-type who likes to do things her own way (Chemistry).
- An applicant feels absolutely called to play guitar on the team (Calling), but he couldn't strum his way out of a paper bag (Craft).
- A candidate seems to be great in most other areas, but she just started attending your church three weeks ago (Connection). She might work out great. But how do you really know?

Second, while you want to bring in people who have all five stars, each of those stars won't burn equally bright. No one's perfect.

So, as you build out these qualification standards and assess new team members, you'll need to decide what are the non-negotiables for each star, and what parts of each star could still be a 'work-in-progress".

Here are each of the Five-Star factors.

Star #1: The Character Factor

> *People with integrity walk safely, but those who follow crooked paths will be exposed.*
>
> Proverbs 10:9

Character involves someone's integrity and spiritual walk. Perfection is not required (obviously). But an intentional pursuit of God is.

Here's the big question you're seeking to answer:

Is this person genuinely pursuing a life of worship that will support their calling to the team?

Star #2: The Craft Factor

> *Then the Lord said to Moses, "Look, I have specifically chosen Bezalel...of the tribe of Judah. I have filled him with the Spirit of God, giving him great wisdom, ability, and expertise in all kinds of crafts.*
>
> Exodus 33

Craft involves a person's…

- Talents, current skills, and experience.
- Commitment to grow and develop their skills.
- Platform presence and expression.

Another "C" word that could be used here is *competency*. But *craft* goes far beyond just being *competent*. You want team members willing to invest in their craft, not just maintain a minimum competency.

Here's the big question you're seeking to answer:

Do they have the skills and experience needed for the role they're applying for, and will they continue to grow and develop those skills?

Remember what we talked about earlier: *talent isn't enough.*

Star #3: The Connection Factor

> *He makes the whole body fit together perfectly. As each part does its own special work, it helps the other parts grow, so that the whole body is healthy and growing and full of love.*
>
> Ephesians 4:16

Connection is the person's commitment and engagement with your church. It's also their potential to be committed to the worship ministry.

Here's the big question you're seeking to answer:

Is this person committed to the overall leadership and direction of our church, as well the worship ministry?

DEEPEN YOUR BENCH

Star #4: The Chemistry Factor

> *They worshiped together at the Temple each day, met in homes for the Lord's Supper, and shared their meals with great joy and generosity–all the while praising God and enjoying the goodwill of all the people.*
>
> Acts 2:46-27

Chemistry is concerned with how well people fit together on the team.

You don't need everyone on the team to be best friends. However, there needs to be respect and camaraderie between members for you to create and maintain a great team culture.

This aspect of qualification is often dismissed as unimportant or secondary. But from experience, I can tell you that people who DON'T connect well with others change the team dynamic significantly – and for the worse.

Here's the big question you're seeking to answer:

Will working and interacting regularly with this person be a positive experience, or a draining one?

Chemistry is the toughest area to qualify. And if you do find later there are chemistry issues, it's even tougher to *disqualify* someone based on it.

In my experience, however, chemistry issues are usually accompanied by deficiencies in one of the other areas:

- There could be issues of pride or a critical spirit (Character).

- They're not plugged in at your church very well (Connection).
- They may have talent for their instrument (Craft), but they prefer a different style and don't want to adapt.
- They're just in the wrong ministry or even the wrong local church (Calling).

Here's the thing, if you have a humble person of good character who's called to your ministry and equipped to do the job, this is someone who can probably get along with your team.

Star #5: The Calling Factor

Therefore I, a prisoner for serving the Lord, beg you to lead a life worthy of your calling, for you have been called by God.

Ephesians 4:1

Calling is another "tough-to-determine" qualifying factor. Essentially you're looking for someone who has a sense that God is leading her to serve in this ministry.

Calling to the worship team isn't a "burning bush" event. It's not on the same level as the calling someone receives to quit their current vocation and go into overseas missions.

Here's the big question you're trying to answer here:

Do I get a sense that God is leading them to serve? (And that word "serve" is really important.)

Here are some additional aspects of *calling* that can help you determine someone's fit.

DEEPEN YOUR BENCH

- *An affirmation of "the call" by leadership.* The leader of the ministry (or church leadership body who approves ministry positions) needs to have the sense that this person is a good fit and is truly being led by the Spirit.
- *An availability that allows the person to serve.* For example, I questioned anyone's "call" to the worship team if they couldn't attend our required midweek rehearsals.
- *An attitude that seeks to honor God and serve his people.* That should be at the heart of their calling. If you don't sense that, there could be an issue.[36]

Since *calling* can be tough to discern, here are some "red flags" to look out for when it comes to being called to the worship team:

- Someone who's insistent that they're *called* despite talent or character issues.
- Someone who believes their gifts and talents are 'evidence of a calling.' *Ability* doesn't equal *calling*.
- Someone who seems to be more about showcasing their talent more than serving the church.

Again, the word "serve" is vital to listen for. But even more crucial, to *look* for.[37]

---

[36] The absence of this attitude may not be a disqualifying factor. Many people don't really understand what's at the heart of serving on the worship team. That's why you have a team member development process.

[37] Look for how a potential new platform team member interacts your production team at auditions. If they treat the techs like "the help," it's game over.

You need to see a humble posture of wanting to serve the church and contribute to the team. And just like we talked about with *Chemistry*, if there's an issue of someone's calling, you'll likely see traces of those issues in the other factors.

One last thing about *calling*.

Sometimes people can't articulate why they want to serve on the team and will say things that raise a yellow flag in your mind. They could still be someone who's a good fit and just needs some training and development.

Remember, not every star is going to shine equally bright.

Building Your Qualification Process

Once you have your philosophy of growth articulated and your standards determined – your definition of a five-star recruit – you're ready to build the *process* that will help you attract, identify, qualify, invite, and acclimate new team members.

We don't have the space in this book to teach the entire process. But let me give you the foundational elements of a healthy and efficient qualification process. I call these the *"The 7 Qs of New Team Member Qualification."*

Here they are:

1. Qualities

As the leader, you must have your standards defined for your worship ministry. That's what the Five Stars are all about.

Once you clearly define your "C" qualities (character, craft, connection, chemistry, and calling), your qualification process will be a systematic exploration to ensure the prospective team member meets those standards.

2. Queue

An amusement park has an organized process to move someone from the end of the line to the end of the ride. (And after about two hours, you know how the children of Israel felt wandering the Sinai desert.)

In the same way, your qualification process needs to move someone systematically from *I'm interested* to *I'm invested*.

If you let someone jump the line (as I did with Jeff), you will miss critical insights into this potential teammate.

This path should include multiple steps (for example – an application, an informal interview, a formal audition, orientation, etc.). And it should involve more than one set of eyes and ears assessing the candidate. (In other words, never audition alone.)

3. Questions

A healthy qualification process has a predetermined list of questions that help you assess the potential team member. You should have specific questions that dig into each of the Five-Star qualities. And you'll need to ask the right questions at the right time in the "Queue."

Not only are the preset questions critical for sniffing out the qualities you want, this list of questions will help you…

- NOT reinvent the wheel each time someone new applies.
- Create a consistent process for every person who goes through your process.
- Delegate parts of the process as you grow in leadership.

4. Quick-Release

A healthy qualification process contains places along the path where people can exit (or be ejected) early on.

If you build your qualification process in the right way, a person may recognize that they're not a good fit and self-select out before you waste his or your time on a needless interview or audition.

Or, you'll see the mismatch in an early step and decide not to move the person on to later steps.

Remember, it's easier to disqualify someone before they join than try to remove them from the team later.

5. Quirks

A healthy qualification process allows for time and interaction to identify the candidate's quirks…

- peculiar behavior
- habits
- personality issues
- musical shortcomings
- etc.

This is important to understand: *Quirks don't necessarily disqualify a person.*

Because let's be real: *we all got our quirks*.

It's just good to know sooner than later what an applicant's quirks might be. If they are *too* quirky, or cross the line towards dysfunction, you'll then need the next Q.

6. Quash

A healthy audition system works to *quash* dysfunctional behavior or unhealthy attitudes before they enter your team.

That is, you have to say NO to people who don't meet your qualification standards – musically, spiritually, or relationally. If you don't say no, that 'bad fit' person will erode the culture of your team.

Remember, your role as team leader is also to be a shepherd. And what do shepherds do besides visit babies born in Bethlehem? (And I think they only did that once.)

They protect the flock.

When you tell someone NO, it isn't about keeping your talent average high. It's about keeping people off your team who aren't a good fit – people who will erode the culture you're trying to build.

Now, if someone isn't entirely qualified, but they aren't deserving of a 'hard pass,' you need the next Q.

7. Qualified Invitation

A successful audition system will leave room for people who aren't yet up to your standards, but they have potential. You can invite them into the team with certain conditions, expectations, or limitations – i.e., a *qualified invitation.*

When you do, be clear about what standards this person needs to work towards. And better still, find someone on your team who can mentor and help move this person along.

If you build these seven Qs into your qualification system correctly, you will create an intentional and relational process that will keep the wrong people out and invite the right people in.

Audition UP!

The last piece of advice I want to give you is one I wish I had followed sooner in my worship leading career.

Audition for who you want, not what you've got.

A woman was trying out to be a vocalist on our team. Let's call her Ana (not her real name).

I had invited one of my experienced BGVs, Julie, to join us. (Julie *is* her real name. If you're reading this, *Hi Julie!)* Within minutes it was clear that Ana just didn't have it.

Her voice had a nice-sounding quality but wasn't very strong. And she struggled to find the right pitch at times. But the most glaring issue was that she couldn't sing harmony.

Shortly before she applied, I had decided to require all BGVs to be able to sing harmony parts.

Since it was just Julie and me interviewing her, I decided to tell her no in that interview rather than delay the conversation to an awkward phone call later in the week. Or worse, schedule an unnecessary full band audition and still have to tell her no.

When telling someone no, I always try to be very specific about where they didn't meet our standards. When I mentioned the inability to sing harmony, she replied, "Well, Lisa can't sing harmony, and she's on the team."

She was right. Lisa (not her real name), along with a couple of other vocalists, were 'melody-only' singers. I had invited them on the team when our standards were different.

DEEPEN YOUR BENCH

It was tough to tell Ana that we had raised our requirement for new vocalists. And no, it wasn't really fair that those other non-harmony singers could be on the team and Ana couldn't. But at that stage in our growth as a team, I no longer needed to fill gaps in our roster. I had more melody-only singers than I could schedule.

And, I didn't want the team held hostage to previous standards. So I made the decision to audition for what we wanted, rather than to get more of what we already had.

And that's not just a skill thing. To deepen your bench in the right way, you need to start being even more selective based on factors that aren't directly tied to talent and skill.

It's going to seem exclusionary to some and unspiritual to others. But remember, you're working to build a team that's leading the gathered worship of your church. It's OK to be selective as long as you prioritize the right qualities.

Grow your team the right way.

If you want to explore how your audition process will help you build a team that makes every Sunday exceptional, schedule an Exceptional Sunday Assessment. During this call, you and a coach will talk about…

- What you'd like your team to look like in the next six, twelve, or eighteen months…
- Where you're at right now with current team members and your pool of potential talent…
- And what might be holding you back from reaching your goals.

Even if you decide it's not the right time or best fit to work with my team, you'll get tremendous amounts of clarity and value from this call.

There's no cost to you for this session, and you can schedule it here:

https://www.worshipteamcoach.com/book-esa

Chapter 19

THE PATH TO TO LOVING BETTER

I feel that there is nothing more truly artistic than to love people.
Vincent Van Gogh

The guys wore matching khaki pants, denim shirts, and striped knit sweater vests. The girls wore denim jumper skirts with white tops and had their bangs teased high.

It was 1993. And we were the coolest traveling college music group in the midwest. I mean, look at us:

(Me, my freshman year–first row, 3rd from the left. I had recently cut off my mullet.)

THE PATH TO TO LOVING BETTER

Even our name was rad: *Celebration!*

I played guitar for this group throughout college. We'd travel to churches on weekends to "minister through music." But we all knew what we were really there for – to drum up business for the college. (Pun intended.)

Thirty years ago, a five-piece band with a six-piece vocal team singing a mix of 90s worship choruses and cheesy, bubblegum-pop Jesus songs was cutting edge for most churches.

More than a few pastors saw our drummer setting up his kit on their platforms and started praying, "Oh dear Jesus, what did I get my church into?!"

But we won over most churches and did a good job of persuading impressionable young high school students to fill out the admission cards.

Because of the worship music surge in the 90s and the contemporary side "winning" the worship war in so many churches, our group evolved from a Christian show choir to more of a modern worship band by my senior year.

The year I was leading the team.

(To every person who served on that team with me that year, I apologize deeply from the bottom of my heart.)

Now, I made a lot of mistakes as the leader of that team. But there's one choice where I knew I made the right decision: *the drummer.*

Unfortunately, our faculty director vetoed my choice. Instead of a rock-solid, experienced drummer who was easy to get along with,[38] he chose a good-looking underclassman with more passion than skill.

Let's just call him *Gary*.

While Gary was passionate about worship, we constantly flew off the rails in rehearsal. These train wrecks were due to his unpredictable tempo.

He also refused to end songs when he was supposed to, pushing us to repeat choruses over and over. Why? Because he wanted to "keep worshiping."

Shortly before our first weekend tour, I pressed the team for an extra rehearsal. "We need more practice," I told them.

"We need to *pray* more!" was Gary's righteously angry reply.

Man, I hated Gary.

As the team's music director, it was my job to get us road ready. I was an insecure 21-year-old with zero leadership experience, so the spiritual side of things took a backseat. I did little to foster the spiritual depth of that team other than to lead us in prayer before rehearsals and performances.

I didn't see how praying longer would magically make our band sound better.

---

[38] Dan Z, if you happen to read this… I'm sorry, brother. I wish I had fought harder for you.

THE PATH TO TO LOVING BETTER

For both Gary and me in those days, *practice* and *prayer*, *work* and *worship*, *musical* and *spiritual* were all binary issues. They were *either-or* propositions.

And it didn't help that Gary and I were both stubborn jackasses.

Unfortunately, I see that same binary thinking with too many worship leaders our coaches work with.

Worship leaders know their teams need to look and sound better, but they also wonder if that pursuit is somehow *unspiritual*.

Or, maybe, the spiritual development of the team should somehow be prioritized *over* musical development efforts.

While that sounds like "the Christian" thing to do, these worship leaders still falsely assume that musical and spiritual development are independent pursuits – or even antithetical to each other.

Because of this, these leaders scour the internet for worship team devotionals and other tools to get their teams to "be more spiritual."

When those tools don't work, or don't work well, these leaders feel guilty because they think they're not doing enough to disciple their team members.

Now, I'm not knocking spiritual growth or worship team devotionals. I've written a lot of team devotionals. And I created an entire training site (WorshipWorkshop.com) with the goal of integrating discipleship into the worship team.

But it's not an either-or proposition. It's both-and: *the journey towards spiritual maturity and musical growth is found on the same path.*

To explore that idea, let's talk about Andragogy.

Andrago-*What?*

I'm not talking about someone who looks like David Bowie. That's a similar-looking word with a much, much different definition.

Andragogy is the study of how adults learn. One of the major principles of adult learning is this: "The Need to Know."

From preschool through college, we learned because we *had* to. None of us had a burning desire to know what a *gerund* is or found our lives enriched when we finally learned about it.

Let's face it, as adults, once we finish with the academic education system, most of us will only seek to learn new skills out of necessity, like for a job or to excel at a passion.

Your worship team is no exception.

With that tenet of adult learning in mind, let's revisit a concept I introduced early.

THE PATH TO TO LOVING BETTER

The Levels of Engagement

Leadership — Invests in others by becoming a guide
Ministry — Worships God *and* serves the congregation
Expression — Confident musicianship *and* Biblical worship
Connection — Connection with the music and other musicians
Survival — Self-absorbed because just trying to get through the song

As I mentioned in Chapter 15, I based the Levels of Engagement on Maslow's Hierarchy of Needs. And similar to Maslow's model, a team member doesn't usually engage in the higher levels until they fulfill the lower ones.

A team member will struggle with the roles in the *Expression*, *Ministry*, and *Leadership* levels if he's still white-knuckling it through a song or failing to connect musically with his fellow instrumentalists or vocal team.

But as a team member progresses to *Expression*, she begins to see that authentic worship and musical excellence are BOTH needed to fulfill the dual platform roles of an engaging lead worshiper: *we worship God and serve the congregation.*

When she hears you say things like, *"Our platform worship will never exceed our private worship,"* it hits her differently at this stage than it did in the *Connection* phase. She now recognizes the *need* to know more about Biblical worship and grow as a worshiper.

I'm not saying you should neglect spiritual or relational development until a team member reaches a certain musical level. In fact, in *Worship Workshop* (http://worshipworkshop.com/), our first two Core Paths that your team members walk through contain foundational Biblical and relational training – along *with* musical development.

The reality is, each of your team members will progress at different rates and have a different propensity toward musical and spiritual growth.

Some will be more like Gary and gravitate towards the spiritual side of serving on a worship team. Others will gravitate toward the musical side.

From what I've experienced, most worship team members fall into the latter group. And that's OK.

Think about how Jesus gathered his disciples and numerous other followers. He didn't enlist them in a spiritual growth program. He met them where they were and used the journey of "life together" to teach them about the Kingdom of Heaven.

Your team members won't be following you down miles of dusty roads. But you and they are on a journey together. Part of that journey is working to improve musically.

Use that practical, external improvement to prepare them for deeper, internal growth. And when they recognize the need, they'll be ready to learn and grow.

THE PATH TO TO LOVING BETTER

The Gateway Drug

We may not like it, but *sounding better* and *looking better* often need to be the "gateway drug" for *loving better*.

Think about it from the perspective of the average worship team member. Most will see the need to improve their ability to sing or play a song long before they recognize they need to engage the congregation.

And later, as they learn to lead the congregation in worship, that will likely trigger an examination of their own worship habits and beliefs.

This isn't always the case. But some leaders reading this book need to be released from the nagging guilt that they're not doing enough to grow their team members spiritually.

If that's you, please hear this: you CAN'T be your worship team members' sole discipler or spiritual mentor. Your team members bear individual responsibility for their own spiritual formation. Your church has a corporate responsibility, too.

So please, cut yourself some slack and realize you can only do so much to advance your team members' walk with God. Instead, embrace the fact that it's a journey that will look different for each team member.

Also, be OK that your discipleship efforts will significantly help some and fall woefully short for others. That's spiritual leadership in any ministry setting.

Stop feeling guilty.

Are you someone who's felt guilty because you're not doing enough "spiritual development." I hope this chapter was good news for you.

If you want to explore how to leverage musical and platform presence training to ultimately grow your team relationally and spiritually, schedule an Exceptional Sunday Assessment. During this call, you and a coach will talk about…

- Where you want your team to grow (spiritually, relationally, AND musically) over the next six to eighteen months…
- Where they're at right now, warts and all – the good, the bad, and the ugly …
- And what might be holding you back from leading them to their next level of engagement.

Even if you decide it's not the right time or best fit to work with my team, you'll get tremendous amounts of clarity and value from this call.

There's no cost to you for this session, and you can schedule it here:

https://www.worshipteamcoach.com/book-esa

The Exciting Conclusion

(OR, JUST THE BEGINNING…?)

Chapter 20

WHEN WILL YOU SKIP EASTER?

No man will make a great leader who wants to do it all himself or get all the credit for doing it.
Andrew Carnegie

This One Particular Easter...

Friend in the lobby after church:
So when was the last time you had an Easter Sunday off?

Me:
Hmm… probably not since the Clinton administration.

In 2018 I (willingly) stepped aside to let my volunteer leaders carry the biggest Sunday of the year. You might wonder why I committed the worship leader equivalent of career suicide.

There were four big reasons I skipped Easter.

1. Absent Father
The first reason is that I've been an almost-absent father and husband during Spring Break for years.

WHEN WILL YOU SKIP EASTER?

Our school system typically schedules Spring Break the week leading up to Easter. As a worship pastor, that typically means no vacation days, leaving my wife as a "spring break single mom" trying to entertain bored kids.

As worship leaders, both the Christmas and Easter seasons take us away from our families – physically away, yes, but also emotionally.

So family was one big reason I stepped away from the platform that Easter.

2. Weariness

The second big reason I took off Easter was that I just needed it. Over the previous years, I've gotten weary of the weekly grind of Sunday after Sunday after Sunday.

I still liked leading worship and loved leading my team. But in full transparency, church music had started feeling more like a widget factory job than a calling to ministry.

This feeling started over two years prior. In late 2016, I fell into a leaderless black hole. All of my volunteer leaders who could carry a Sunday had left.

- One moved out of state for a job.
- One took a long, personal hiatus.
- Another left to fill an interim position at another church.

As a result, I led every week for a big chunk of the year without a Sunday off. You might think, no big deal, Jon. I lead 53 out of 52 Sundays at my church.

But you have to understand. By then, I had tasted the sweet fruits of "triple time off" that I talked about in Chapter 10. I realized how much I needed that space and rest.

3. Working ON vs. IN

That's also when I discovered this truth: It's tough to *lead the ministry* when I *lead on Sunday.*

When I was planning, preparing, and leading Sunday services, there was not enough time and energy left to think, dream, read, plan, mentor, develop, shepherd, train, etc.

Things only got worse when I reduced my hours to half-time at my church to give more attention to WorshipTeamCoach.com. I realized that I needed 'off-platform' weeks if I wanted to grow leaders and develop effective ministry systems.

I couldn't work on my team's long-term growth while learning guitar riffs and the melody to a new pre-service song.

So, part of taking Easter off was giving myself space to work ON the ministry versus IN it.

4. Substitute Worship Leader

The fourth reason I took off Easter Sunday was that I needed to get serious about leadership development and succession.

There's a holy day on the liturgical calendar just after the Advent season known as Youth Pastor Sunday.[39] It's that sparsely attended Sunday after Christmas – a preaching purgatory between the last

---

[39] OK, Youth Pastor Sunday is not really on the liturgical calendar. But it should be. Who do we talk to about getting that added – *the Episcopalians?*

WHEN WILL YOU SKIP EASTER?

Advent message and the Sunday after New Year's *"rah rah let's be better Christians this year"* series.

The conversation among church leaders goes something like this:

"The senior pastor needs a break. Who can fill in?"

"The youth pastor could."

"But what if he bombs?"

"Meh, no one's here anyway."

We joke about it. But as worship leaders, that's how we treat our volunteer leaders. As *substitutes!*

"I'm on vacation. Can you cover me?"

Or…

"I've got a conference in November. Want to lead?"

Or…

"Sunday's on the 4th of July. You free to step up?"

This approach causes two problems:

1. We're training *substitutes*, not leaders.

Filling in on Sunday might be a beneficial way to stretch a newer leader. But if we want high-capacity leaders, we must challenge them beyond occasional Sunday subbing.

2. We're creating a cult of personality.

The North American church is riddled with celebrity-status teaching pastors and worship leaders. It doesn't just occur in high-profile megachurches. The cult of personality happens even in the smallest churches.

How many times have you heard this "compliment" after taking a Sunday off: *"I'm so glad you're back. Worship just wasn't as good without you last week."*

Early in ministry, that stroked my ego. Now, it breaks my heart.

If we're serious about being E4 leaders – incorporating the ancient leadership wisdom Ephesians 4:11-12 – we have to make bold changes like I've outlined in this book.

First, we need to stop doing the work of ministry ourselves and start equipping others.

Second, we need to throw off the celebrity leader status and begin doing the selfless work of letting other leaders take our place in the spotlight. (And not just when we're on vacation.)

Abdicating my upfront leadership role on Easter was about way more than needing a break.

By early 2018, I had rebuilt my platform leadership team.

So it was time to put up or shut up.

I needed to proclaim this to my team, my church, and myself:

"Leading leaders is more important than leading on the platform."

And guess what *didn't* happen on that Easter Sunday I didn't lead?

No one said to me after our service, "Gosh, that would've been better if you had been up there."

Not one person.

WHEN WILL YOU SKIP EASTER?

My volunteer leaders did a fantastic job leading us musically and helping us worship the resurrected King.

Other than my friend who'd asked me how long it had been since I'd led on Easter, no one commented on my platform absence.

It was a non-event.

That's how much we had moved to a place of E4 leadership. And along the way, we built a team that made every Sunday exceptional, no matter who was scheduled.

Including me!

You might not be in a place to take off one of the "big Sundays." No worries. I didn't start there. (Nor do I recommend it.) But what's your next step to move towards leading leaders more and leading on the platform less?

And, when's your "not leading on Easter" line in the sand?

It might not be Easter Sunday. But set a target date to NOT lead for a future significant Sunday and still be in attendance.

And let me know when it is and what your livestream link is. I'm looking forward to NOT seeing you!

(Seriously, send me an email jon@worshipteamcoach.com and let me know about your first, big "skipped Sunday" so I can celebrate it with you.)

Schedule any Sunday off you want.

If you want to explore how to grow as a leader of leaders and have the freedom to schedule yourself any Sunday off, book an Exceptional Sunday Assessment. During this call, you and a coach will talk about…

- What you want your worship ministry to look like in the next six to eighteen months…
- Where you're at right now with leadership development and taking intentional time off…
- And what might be holding you back from reaching your goals.

Even if you decide it's not the right time or best fit to work with my team, you'll get tremendous amounts of clarity and value from this call.

There's no cost to you for this session, and you can schedule it here:

https://www.worshipteamcoach.com/book-esa

Chapter 21

SERIOUSLY, WHAT'S NEXT??

Be willing to be uncomfortable. Be comfortable being uncomfortable. It may get tough, but it's a small price to pay for living a dream.
Peter McWilliams

As I wrap this book, I want to revisit the promise I made to you at the beginning.

I promised to show you what it takes to build a worship team that makes every Sunday exceptional. I did that as best as I could in a book short enough for the average worship leader.

Can I tell you a secret? Christian book publishers do not consider worship leaders to be "avid readers." Big surprise, huh?

That's why relatively few books for worship leaders are traditionally published – and why I tried to keep this book short. (I said, *"tried."*)

Another promise I made was to get you results in advance.

I packed as much practical and tactical stuff in the book as possible while, here again, keeping it short enough for the average worship leader to finish.

SERIOUSLY, WHAT'S NEXT??

But here's the question: *results in advance of what?*

In advance of you deciding to work with my team. I was clear in the beginning that my team and I would love to have the opportunity to help you improve your worship ministry.

We want to help you build a team that makes every Sunday exceptional…

- No matter who's scheduled…
- Without burning out you or your team, and…
- At a pace that would be almost impossible on your own.

You can make tremendous improvements in your worship ministry on your own if you apply this book.

BUT… 'going it alone' comes at a cost.

When you invite my team along on your leadership journey, we will help you…

- Get clarity about which areas of your ministry to focus on first.
- Create a clear plan to improve your team (and get their buy-in for true change).
- Free up 2, 3, or even 4 hours a week to rest or reinvest into your family, self, or ministry.
- Tackle ministry improvements in short work cycles to avoid overwhelm and track your progress.
- Get motivated and stay accountable to get the work *done*.
- Make critical changes more quickly with our ready-to-implement processes and done-for-you tools.

- Have confidence that you're on the right track – and know how and when to pivot when you're not.

The next step to explore working with us is to schedule a short one-on-one session called the Exceptional Sunday Assessment.

During this call we'll...

- Take a look at how well your team is producing excellent Sundays, and we'll see what's working and what's not.
- Identify areas where you can raise your team's standard of excellence on and off the platform over the next 90 days and beyond.
- Uncover the #1 issue holding your team back from sounding fantastic and leading engaging worship consistently.
- Develop a 3-step action plan that will help you make every Sunday exceptional ASAP.

During this first call, there is nothing to buy and no pressure.[40] It's about discovering where you're at, where you want to go, and what might be holding you back.

There's no cost to you for this session, but we do ask you commit to three things:

- Complete a short, pre-call assessment.
- Watch a brief video that will help you get more out of this session.

---

[40] We don't do "pressure" during *any* step of this discovery process. We want to be a help to worship leaders and churches. So it's about finding a good fit for you, whether that's our coaching program or another resource or product we might have. And if we're not a good fit, we'll tell you.

- Show up on time and ready to dig in with the coach.

Even if you decide we're not the best fit for you, you'll still get tons of clarity, insight, and a simple plan you can run with on your own.

Here's how to sign up for this no-cost-to-you call.

1. Go to this page (worshipteamcoach.com/book-esa) and select the day and time that works for you.
2. Complete the form.
3. Mark your calendar and show up on time and ready to go.

My team and I are looking forward to getting to know you and discovering how we can help you build a team that's exceptional every Sunday.

I can't wait to help you build the kind of worship ministry you've always dreamed of leading.

ABOUT THE AUTHOR

Jon Nicol lives and works in the middle of Ohio with his wife Shannon and their four kids. They enjoy spontaneous dance parties to end credit music and eating ice cream. (Sometimes at the same time.)

Jon served as a vocational worship pastor for 19+ years. After his first decade in ministry, he discovered his knack for using his many mistakes to help other worship leaders. In 2009, he founded WorshipTeamCoach.com.

Since then, he and his team have had the privilege to serve thousands of worship leaders in six continents through books, articles, training products, and coaching.[41]

---

[41] It's Antarctica… in case you were wondering which continent we haven't served yet. We're still looking for that elusive South Pole worship leader.

Printed in Great Britain
by Amazon